DESEGREGATION IN
HIGHER EDUCATION

DESEGREGATION IN HIGHER EDUCATION

Samuel L. Myers Sr., Ph.D.

Editor

A NAFEO Research Institute Publication Supported By
Grants From
The Carnegie Corporation,
The Charles Stewart Mott Foundation,
The Pew Memorial Trust Company,
and The Rockefeller Foundation.

UNIVERSITY
PRESS OF
AMERICA

Lanham • New York • London

Copyright © 1989 by the

NAFEO Research Institute

University Press of America,® Inc.

4720 Boston Way
Lanham, MD 20706

3 Henrietta Street
London WC2E 8LU England

Printed in the United States of America

British Cataloging in Publication Information Available

Co-published by arrangement with The National
Association for Equal Opportunity in Higher Education

Library of Congress Cataloging–in–Publication data

Desegregation in higher education / Samuel L. Myers, Sr., editor.
p.   cm.
1. College integration– –United States– –History. 2. Afro–American
universities and colleges– –History. I Myers, Samuel L. II. NAFEO
Research Institute (U.S.)
LC212.72.D48   1988   88–39407 CIP
370.19'342– –dc19
ISBN 0–8191–7290–1 (alk. paper).
ISBN 0–8191–7291–X   (pbk. : alk. paper)

All University Press of America books are produced on acid-free paper.
The paper used in this publication meets the minimum requirements of American
National Standard for Information Sciences—Permanence of Paper for Printed Library
Materials, ANSI Z39.48–1984.   ∞

Table of Contents

Foreword

Public Policy concerning the education of blacks falls into distinct stages. Initially, laws *PROHIBITED* the education of blacks. Following the Civil War the *DEVELOPMENT* of educational institutions to provide rudimentary revival skills to the newly freed slaves was encouraged. Public policy soon shifted, however, to one of *SEGREGATION* of institutions into those for blacks and whites. Following the determination in 1954 by the Supreme Court of the unconstitutionality of the separate but equal doctrine, public policy shifted to that of *DESEGREGATION*.

In a sense, public policy for the past 34 years has represented a quest for desegregation. However, motivations and strategies have changed in face of unexpected impediments and demographic shifts. Initially, the emphasis was literally on desegregation, dismantling a dual system of education, assimilating black students into white institutions and increasing the enrollment of white students at the historically black colleges and universities (HBCUs), and removing the racial identifiability of institutions. Writing in Chapter I, the writer indicated that when it became apparent that the deseg-regation policy directed toward dismantling a dual system of education would weaken or eliminate black colleges and thereby hurt black students, to whose education historically black colleges were disproportionately contributing, public policy shifted to that of *ENHANCEMENT* of the historically black colleges and universities. When it became apparent in the early 80's that black educational progress had peaked in the mid-70's at the same time that blacks and other minorities were becoming an increasing precentage of the work force, renewed attention was focused on improving access, retention and graduation of minorities into colleges and universities. We have designated this as *INTERGRATION.*

Recent studies and strategies have focused primarily on increasing the enrollment and retention of black students at predominantly white institutions. This taken together with recent court decisions that relieved the Office for Civil Rights of the responsibility of enforcing states to develop and implement desegregation plans could, if the decision is upheld on appeal, have serious implications for the continued enhancement and viability of the historically black colleges and universities. This could well become a stage of disintegration for these institutions. Since the last three stages of public policy concerning the education of Blacks, *Desegregation, Enhancement* and *Integration,* are in reality variations on a common theme, it is appropriate that we devote this volume to a discussion of desegregation issues.

In Chapter II, Dr. Julia Wells begins by discussing individual and institutional racism and indicates that although both render harmful injustices in our society, institutional racism is more prevasive in that ". . . institutional racism is harmful not only to blacks who are targets, but also erodes the core of idealism and progress in American society." She concludes her discussion by recommending strategies for combating racism in higher education.

In a survey of desegregation activities at Maryland's historically black public institutions for undergraduate higher education. Dr. Paul Fairley surveyed the perceptions of key HBCU administratior toward the adequacy of enhancement resources and the effectiveness of desegregation activities. The consensus was that although Maryland has undertaken substantive actions to enhance its public black colleges, more needs to be done. The study offers recommendations to various state agencies, the federal government, and other policy makers which should be helpful in eliminating vestiges of a dual higher education system.

Dr. Tomlinson presents the findings from a survey questionnaire, distributed to the six key administrators at each of the 34 majority institutions in the University System of Georgia Higher Education, designed to examine the administrators' responses to the issues of recruiting and retaining black American faculty. The survey findings indicate that "from an attitutional perspective, an overwhelming majority of administrators surveyed indicate that they are either in favor of increasing the number of black faculty, perceive other administrators to be in favor or actively recruiting black faculty, or perceive such recruitment to be appropriate. They acknowledge, by an overwhelming majority, that the numbers of black faculty do not exceed sufficiency." Recommendations are then given for recruiting and retaining black American faculty at the majority universities in Georgia.

Samuel L. Myers, Sr.
NAFEO

Chapter 1

Black Colleges
from Prohibition, Encouragement, and
Segregation
to Desegregation and Enhancement and
Integration

Dr. Samuel L. Myers, Sr.
President
NAFEO

In order to understand better the current situation and prospects for improving the education of blacks in the future, it might be well to review the five stages through which public policy concerning the education of blacks has passed.

The first stage was one of *PROHIBITION*. Prior to the end of the Civil War there were strict laws in the southern states prohibiting the teaching of blacks to read and write. The motivations for the enactment of such restric-

1

tive legislation were undoubtedly traceable to fears of slave uprisings and the desire to stifle yearnings for freedom and to keep slaves subjugated to work on menial, unpleasant tasks. The obsession to deny education to slaves indirectly and implicitly indicated a recognition by the power structure of the contributions education could potentially make to the advancement of a people.

The second stage of public policy with respect to the education of blacks—*DEVELOPMENT*—ensued after the end of the Civil War in 1865. This was a period of active development and promotion of education for blacks. The Freedman's Bureau, religious organizations, philanthropists and even newly freed slaves themselves actively established schools for blacks and promoted education for blacks. The emphasis was primarily on providing rudimentary survival skills for blacks. Nevertheless, the result was an unprecedented expansion of educational opportunities. Most of the historically black colleges and universities (HBCUs) in existence today were established or trace their roots to educational institutions that were established during this period.

This third stage was that of *SEGREGATION*. Following the Hayes/Tildon dispute in 1876, the compromise to withdraw Federal troops from the South, the end of reconstruction, and, finally, the *Plessy vs. Ferguson Decision in 1896,* segregation of the races was firmly entrenched by custom, by law and by constitutional interpretation. Theoretically, blacks were to have been accorded equal though separate success to public accommodations. In practice, in every aspect of public life, from public utilities to public colleges, separation of the races was rigidly enforced but the requirement of equal treatment was universally violated. The black colleges proved to be the key in attacking this legally enforced segregation and inequality. Recently, a group of Brazilian blacks, supported by the Ford Foundation, identified a lack of education as the major factor contributing to their plight in Brazil, where literacy is a prerequisite for voting and where most of the blacks are illiterate. The study group concluded that a model to be emulated was the black college in the United States. The historically black colleges, indeed, though segregated and under-funded, succeeded in producing a solid middle-class among blacks. These college educated blacks, chafing under the indignities of segregation vowed and acted to be set free.

The National Association for the Advancement of Colored People (NAACP), with expert involvement of black educators, particularly the professors of the black law schools, challenged the separate but equal doctrine in the courts. Victories in the 1930's were consistently won. The evidence was irrefutable. Though blacks were taxed equitably, black schools and colleges were not accorded equitable support from tax funds. States in the 1940's, in their desperation to keep the educational institutions for blacks and whites separate and segregated, hastily implemented schemes to make it appear that the systems were equal. Scholarships were given to black students to go out of state to professional schools to prevent them from enrolling in in-state professional schools, such as those of law and medicine. In other cases, graduate schools and law schools were hastily appended to existing black colleges to provide advance education to black students in-state. In the end, these efforts were to no avail. The Supreme Court, in its *Brown vs. Board of Education Decision in 1954,* struck down legally condoned segregation in publicly supported institutions. The Supreme Court, by approving the implementation of desegregation remedies "with all deliberate speed," effectively extended the desegregation period until 1964 when the Civil Rights Act was enacted. This ushered in a fourth stage of public policy toward the education of black, *DESEGREGATION.*

From 1964 to 1976 the conventional wisdom among policymakers, including many Federal administrators, foundation heads, corporate donors and even large numbers of middle class blacks themselves, was that policies should be implemented to increase the enrollment of black students at predominantly white colleges and universities, increase the white presence on black campuses and to eradicate the racial identity of educational institutions. In essence, the education of blacks was to be shifted from the historically black colleges to predominantly white institutions. This appeared logical. To gain access to white institutions is what blacks had been fighting for. The sleek new campuses of flagship universities, with their diversified curricula and well-paid faculty, should assure a higher quality education. Furthermore, the Civil Rights Act of 1964 required public colleges and universities to implement affirmative action plans to attract more blacks or face the threat of losing Federal funding. When it appeared that state institutions were dragging their feet, blacks themselves, through the Legal Defense Fund, filed suit in Federal court—the "Adams case—to prod the Office for Civil Rights to obtain acceptable plans from states to dismantle their dual system of education and if such acceptable plans were not forthcoming, to cut off Federal funds.

For a while, it appeared that desegregation policies were paying off with respect to expanding educational opportunities for blacks. Concurrent with the implementation of these policies was the most dramatic expansion

4

of black enrollment in postsecondary education in history. Between the mid-sixties and the mid-seventies the enrollment of blacks in postsecondary education doubled. By the mid-seventies, black and white high school graduates were matriculating in college at approximately the same rate. The desegregation policy appeared to be causing improvements in the education of blacks, but, then, was it?

Closer examination revealed that progress had not been so favorable as the data initially indicated. Only a small percentage of black students were enrolled at the prestigious private universities and the flagship public universities. A large percentage of students who enrolled at predominantly white institutions matriculated but did not actually graduate. The attrition rate for blacks at predominantly white colleges and universities was disproportionately high. A large percentage of the black students enrolled in postsecondary education were really enrolled in community colleges and disproportionately in terminal programs. They, accordingly, were not candidates for transfer to baccalaureate programs that are generally a prerequisite for top management and professsional positions. Furthermore, the expansion of black students at white universities did not represent a reallocation of black students from historically black colleges to predominantly white institutions. The historically black colleges were increasing their enrollment, though at a slower rate, *concurrently* with the increase in enrollment of black students at white institutions. It is now clear in retrospect that the phenomenal growth in the enrollment of black students during the late 60's and early 70's was traceable to a significant increase in the population of blacks, particularly in the college age cohorts, and the rapid expansion of Federal support for education, particularly the expansion and availability of student financial aid to low-income students.

During the mid-seventies, the Supreme Court Decisions, in such cases as the Bakke Case, dampened the enthusiasm of white universities to implement affirmative action programs. The population growth slowed. Inflation soared. Thus, universities, facing fiscal deficits, were less enthusiastic about offering scholarships to black students, hiring additional black faculty or implementing costly black studies programs. The experiment with DESEGREGATION also proved costly in human terms. Large numbers of able students were induced to enter predominantly white institutions only to discover that they were in a hostile environment, unwanted, uncared for and buffeted by racism. They left prematurely, never to complete their education, inspite of their great academic potential.

There are quantitative data to indicate that progress in the education of blacks stalled in the mid-seventies and that the momentum has not been regained since that time. The major loss has been in enrollment. Black student enrollment has dropped from 9.4 percent of the approximately eleven million students in all higher education institutions in 1976 to 8.8 percent of the approximately twelve million in 1984. More black students are going to community colleges, from 41.5 percent in 1976 to 42.7 percent in 1984. During the late sixties and early seventies there was a steady increase in the percentage of blacks graduating from high school and an increase in the percentage of black high school graduates enrolling in college. Since then, there has been an increase in the percentage of blacks graduating from high school but a reduction in the percentage of these black high school graduates enrolling in college. There has been a precipitous decline (21 percent) of blacks earning the master's degree. Given the disproportionately high mortality and morbidity rates among blacks, medical educators in the 1960's set as a goal the increase of the percentage of blacks enrolled in medical school to a proportion somewhat equivalent to the percentage of blacks in the total population (approximately 10 percent). The enrollment, in fact, did increase swiftly from a level of 2.7 percent in the late-sixties of 7.2 percent in the early seventies, a peak from which it receded to approximately six percent, where it has persisted through 1985. The percentage of blacks enrolled in law school appears to have reached equilibrium at an even lower level, approximately 4.7 percent, where it has remained for a decade. The decline in the production of black Ph.D.'s has also declined. This decline in turn is undoubtedly related to the decline in black faculty. Whereas white faculty increased between 1975 and 1983 from approximately 447,000 to 487,000, black faculty, which stood at 19,746 in 1975, actually dropped by 115 in 1983. It is only in retrospect that we can now document statistically the damaging impact of the desegregation experiment in public policy between 1964 and 1976.

Even prior to 1976, however, the stage was being set for the conceptualization and implementation of a new policy stage concerning the education of blacks: *EN-HANCEMENT*. It started with Attorney Herbert Reid, Charles Hamilton Houston Distinguished Professor of Law at Howard University and General Counsel to NA-FEO. Attorney Reid discerned the potentially destructive impact on the black colleges in taking a desegregation policy to its logical extremes. Setting as an ultimate goal the shifting of black students to predominantly white institutions and increasing the white enrollment at black colleges would end in the merging or closing of the black colleges. Since historically black colleges were contributing disproportionately to the education of blacks and since, furthermore, many white institutions had experienced dismal failure and demonstrated a lack of commitment to educating blacks, the desegregation policy would, if it succeeded, cause the demise of black colleges and lead to a diminution of educational opportunities for black. The starting point, Reid argued, should be to enhance educational opportunities for blacks. This would lead logically to enhancing the historically black colleges, given their proven track record in educating blacks. Indeed, given the fact that approximately 100 black colleges produce almost as many baccalaureate recipients among blacks as do 3,000 white institutions and given the fact that these graduates help to people the professions in the broader society in which blacks are consistently underrepresented, the black colleges become an instrument for integrating the broader society rather than being themselves an anachronistic relic of segregation.

In 1973 NAFEO, guided by Attorney Reid's counsel, filed an *amicus curiae* brief in the Adams case. The courts ruled that the Office for Civil Rights, in approving statewide desegregation plans, should assure that the special needs of historically black colleges be considered and that an undue burden of desegregation not be placed on the historically black colleges. This began a process of policy formulation to enhance the historically black colleges.

The legislative sector adopted the enhancement policy. In the Reauthorization Act of 1985, Representative Augustus Hawkins and Senator Paul Simon sponsored and Congress enacted into law the Historically Black College

Act which authorized a setaside of 100 million dollars exclusively for the institutional development of historically black colleges. Similarly, Congressman William Gray was successful in spearheading legislation requiring a ten percent setaside of the appropriations of the United States Agency for International Development for minority businesses, voluntary organizations and Historically Black Colleges. A goal of five percent of Defense appropriations for minority businesses and black colleges has also been established by Congress. The Congressional Black Caucus has established a Setaside Committee under the chairmanship of Congressman Mervyn Dymally to expand the legislative application of the setaside to promote the enhancement of historically black colleges.

The Executive branch of the Federal Government has also endorsed the policy of enhancement of the historically black colleges and black higher education. President Jimmy Carter, before leaving office, signed an Executive Order directing Federal agencies to increase their support to the historically black colleges. President Reagan, on September 15, 1981, issued an even stronger Executive Order (#12320) directing Federal agencies and requesting the private sector to enhance the historically black colleges. On September 22, 1982, President Reagan issued a supplement to the Executive Order to improve the Administration's implementation, monitoring and evaluation of his Executive Order on the black colleges. A White House Initiative Office on the Historically Black Colleges and Universities was established and staffed with strong leadership to work with Federal agencies in establishing goals and in preparing reports on actual funding obligations to the black colleges. In recent years, the White House Initiative Office has focused on the problem of the underrepresentation of blacks in science and technology. The office has mobilized support from among the leadership in the private sector to address this problem.

It is now becoming clear that since 1986, public policy with respect to the education of blacks has entered a new stage: *INTEGRATION*. The emphasis is on counteracting the decline in the overall participation of blacks in postsecondary education and to increase the rates of matriculation, retention and graduation of blacks, not only in two-year and four-year colleges but in graduate and professional schools as well. Unlike the desegregation or assimilation policies of the 1960s, the underlying motivation is not to achieve justice or provide reparation to blacks for past legally condoned injustices and not to penalize or threaten majority institutions for perpetuating segregation. Rather, current efforts are based on a recognition that blacks and other minorities will constitute a significant percentage—up to forty percent by the 1990s—of U.S. population. Accordingly, if this nation is to be economically competitive, militarily strong and democratically tranquil, it must develop this significant pool of potential talent. There is another major difference between the new stage and the desegregation period. In the past, the emphasis was on dismantling segregation by increasing the percentage of black students on predominantly white campuses and increasing the percentage of white students at historically black colleges. This salt and pepper approach stressed reallocation of blacks and whites to desegregate educational institutions. The current emphasis is on increasing the flow, the aggregate supply of blacks in higher education. It may well be that the policy is one of true integration. Tables 1–6 present the Fall 1986 black and white student enrollment in the

10

NAFEO member institutions; and the historically and predominantly black colleges that are now closed.

The American Council on Education (ACE), the major coordinating association for postsecondary education in America, with a membership of approximately 1,500 colleges and universities, has accorded high priority to minority concerns. Through its Office for Minority Concerns, an Advisory Committee to that Office, a special Task Force of the Board of Directors and the Board of Directors itself, the American Council on Education has outlined a program to address the issues of racism, minority enrollment, retention and graduation and the formulation of public policies on minority education. In addition, ACE is in the process of publishing handbooks to provide technical assistance to campuses in planning and implementing strong minority oriented activities. The Council devoted a significant segment of its January 1988 National Conference on Higher Education to minority issues.

The American Council on Education has also established a Committee on Minority Participation in Postsecondary Education in the Washington Higher Education Secretariat, which consists of heads of the major associations representing most of the colleges and universities in the United States. This Committee is currently sharing ideas on problems and successful programs in enrolling and retaining minority students from the vantage point of diverse types of institutions.

The American Council on Education's efforts constitute one of a number of a growing list of activities now being focused on various facets of black postsecondary enrollment. The National Association of Independent Colleges and Universities (NAICU) recently concluded a

11

TABLE 1
Percent of Black and White Students Enrolled in Historically Black Colleges and Universities, Fall 1986
NAFEO Membership (N = 104)

State/Institutions	Date Estab.	Control/*** Level	Total Students	Black Total	Black Percent	White Total	White Percent
ALABAMA							
**Alabama A&M University	1875	PU-4+G	4,045	3,039	75.1	238	5.9
Alabama State University	1874	PU-4+G	3,540	3,451	97.5	24	0.7
S. D. Bishop State Jr. College	1936	PU-2	1,664	1,338	80.4	306	18.4
Concordia College	1922	PR-2	410	401	97.8	0	0.0
*Lawson State Community College	1949	PU-2	1,522	1,509	99.1	13	0.8
*Miles College	1905	PR-4	456	443	97.1	1	0.2
Oakwood College	1896	PR-4	1,000	888	88.8	0	0.0
Selma University	1878	PR-2	206	206	100.0	0	0.0
Stillman College	1876	PR-4	793	764	96.3	2	0.3
*Talladega College	1867	PR-4	442	437	98.9	1	0.2
**Tuskegee University	1881	PR-4+GP	3,070	2,718	88.5	103	3.4
ARKANSAS							
Arkansas Baptist College	1884	PR-4	233	225	96.6	8	3.4
Philander Smith College	1877	PR-4	572	489	85.5	4	0.7
Shorter College	1886	PR-2	120	99	82.5	13	10.8
**University of Arkansas	1873	PU-4	2,900	2,321	80.0	567	19.6

DELAWARE							
**Delaware State College	1891	PU-4	2,327	1,253	53.8	1,000	43.0
DISTRICT OF COLUMBIA							
Howard University	1867	PR-4+GP	11,053	8,805	79.7	171	1.5
**University of the District of Columbia	1851	PU-4+G	11,098	9,897	89.2	556	5.0
FLORIDA							
Bethune-Cookman College	1904	PR-4	1,815	1,711	94.3	16	0.9
*Edward Waters College	1866	PR-4	712	667	93.7	10	1.4
**Florida A&M University	1887	PU-4+G	5,377	4,429	82.4	678	12.6
Florida Memorial College	1879	PR-4	2,172	1,797	82.7	5	0.2
GEORGIA							
Albany State College	1903	PU-4+G	1,754	1,463	83.4	282	16.1
Atlanta University	1865	PR-G	1,072	833	77.7	12	1.1
Clark College	1869	PR-4	1,883	1,850	98.2	0	0.0
**Fort Valley State College	1895	PU-4+G	1,811	1,656	91.4	118	6.5
Morehouse College	1867	PR-4	2,121	2,066	97.4	0	0.0
Morehouse School of Medicine	1981	PR-GP	132	101	76.5	16	12.1
*Morris Brown College	1881	PR-4	1,086	1,065	98.1	0	0.0
Paine College	1882	PR-4	789	724	91.8	44	5.6
Savannah State College	1890	PU-4+G	1,694	1,330	78.5	303	17.9
*Spelman College	1881	PR-4	1,586	1,550	97.7	0	0.0

13

TABLE 1 (Continued)

State/Institutions	Date Estab.	Control/*** Level	Total Students	Black Total	Black Percent	White Total	White Percent
KENTUCKY							
**Kentucky State University	1886	PU-4+G	2,205	895	40.6	1,266	57.4
Simmons University Bible College	1873	PR-4	99	99	100	0	0.0
LOUISIANA							
Dillard University	1869	PR-4	1,275	1,266	99.3	1	0.1
Grambling State University	1901	PU-4+G	5,224	4,984	95.4	71	1.4
**Southern University (Baton Rouge)	1880	PU-4+GP	9,110	8,000	87.8	375	4.1
Southern University (New Orleans)	1956	PU-4+G	3,302	2,868	86.9	251	7.6
Southern University (Shreveport)	1964	PU-2	756	725	95.9	31	4.1
Xavier University	1925	PR-4+G	1,992	1,800	90.4	143	7.2
MARYLAND							
Bowie State College	1865	PU-4+G	2,902	1,668	57.5	942	32.5
Coppin State College	1900	PU-4+G	2,315	2,000	86.4	80	3.5
Morgan State University	1867	PU-4+G	3,702	3,130	84.5	170	4.6
**University of Maryland, Eastern Shore	1886	PU-4+G	1,259	920	73.1	257	20.4

MISSISSIPPI							
**Alcorn State University	1871	PU-4+G	2,319	2,245	96.8	103	4.4
Coahoma Jr. College	1949	PU-2	1,362	1,339	98.3	23	1.7
Jackson State University	1877	PU-4+G	6,319	5,858	92.7	150	2.4
Mary Holmes College	1892	PR-2	345	336	97.4	1	0.3
*Mississippi Valley State University	1950	PU-4+G	2,344	2,330	99.4	7	0.3
Natchez Jr. College	1885	PR-2	107	107	100	0	0
Prentiss Institute Jr. College	1907	PR-2	124	124	100	0	0
Rust College	1866	PR-4	915	893	97.6	4	0.4
Tougaloo College	1869	PR-4	902	890	98.7	12	1.3
*Utica Jr. College	1903	PU-2	640	632	98.8	5	0.8
MISSOURI							
Harris-Stowe State College	1857	PU-4	1,374	983	71.5	344	25.0
**Lincoln University	1866	PU-4+G	2,486	772	31.1	1600	64.4
NORTH CAROLINA							
Barber-Scotia College	1867	PR-4	383	382	99.7	1	0.3
*Bennett College	1873	PR-4	576	574	99.7	2	0.3
Elizabeth City State University	1891	PU-4	1,615	1,321	81.8	283	17.5
Fayetteville State University	1877	PU-4+G	2,921	2,173	74.4	679	23.2
Johnson C. Smith University	1867	PR-4	1,130	1,105	97.8	0	0.0
Livingstone College	1879	PR-4	733	712	97.1	4	0.5
**North Carolina A&T State University	1891	PU-4+G	5,966	4,978	83.4	705	11.8

TABLE 1 (Continued)

State/Institutions	Date Estab.	Control/*** Level	Total Students	Black		White	
				Total	Percent	Total	Percent
North Carolina Central University	1910	PU-4+G	4,988	4,113	82.5	804	16.1
Saint Augustine's College	1867	PR-4	1,636	1,636	100.0	0	0.0
*Shaw University	1865	PR-4	1,742	1,373	78.8	17	1.0
Winston-Salem State University	1892	PU-4	2,570	2,187	85.1	388	15.1
OHIO							
Central State University	1856	PU-4	2,670	2,358	88.3	230	8.6
Wilberforce University	1856	PR-4	797	794	99.6	2	0.3
OKLAHOMA							
**Langston University	1897	PU-4	2,030	968	47.7	841	41.4
PENNSYLVANIA							
Cheyney University	1837	PU-4+G	1,507	1,437	95.4	0	0.0
*Lincoln University	1854	PU-4	1,245	1,111	89.2	98	7.9
SOUTH CAROLINA							
Allen University	1870	PR-4	233	219	94.0	14	6.0
Benedict College	1870	PR-4	1,510	1,453	96.2	16	1.1
Claflin College	1869	PR-4	757	747	98.7	3	0.4

16

Institution	Year	Type					
*Clinton Jr. College	1994	PR-2	95	95	100.0	0	0.0
Denmark Technical College	1948	PU-2	689	652	94.6	32	4.6
Morris College	1908	PR-4	675	674	99.9	1	0.1
**South Carolina State College	1896	PU-4+G	3,869	3,570	92.3	261	6.7
Voorhees College	1897	PR-4	576	571	99.1	0	0.0
TENNESSEE							
Fisk University	1866	PR-4+G	538	509	94.6	1	0.2
Knoxville College	1875	PR-4	436	393	90.1	30	6.9
Lane College	1882	PR-4	531	529	99.6	2	0.4
*LeMoyne-Owen College	1862	PR-4	844	827	98.0	0	0.0
Meharry Medical College	1876	PR-GP	678	534	78.8	39	5.8
Morristown College	1881	PR-2	178	176	98.9	2	1.1
**Tennessee State University	1912	PU-4+G	6,737	4,263	63.3	2,141	31.8
TEXAS							
Bishop College	1881	PR-4	946	608	64.3	0	0.0
Huston-Tillotson College	1876	PR-4	520	327	62.9	5	1.0
*Jarvis Christian College	1912	PR-4	533	531	99.6	1	0.2
Paul Quinn College	1872	PR-4	464	444	95.7	11	2.4
**Prairie View A&M University	1876	PU-4	4,499	3,658	81.3	399	8.9
Southwestern Christian College	1949	PR-2	251	226	90.0	2	0.8
Texas College	1894	PR-4	478	356	74.5	1	0.2
Texas Southern University	1947	PU-4+G	7,246	5,320	73.4	181	2.5
*Wiley College	1873	PR-4	537	503	93.7	1	0.2

TABLE 1 (Continued)

State/Institutions	Date Estab.	Control/*** Level	Total Students	Black Total	Black Percent	White Total	White Percent
VIRGIN ISLANDS							
University of the Virgin Islands	1962	PU-4+G	2,495	1,911	76.6	222	8.9
VIRGINIA							
Hampton University	1868	PR-4+G	4,482	4,186	93.4	228	5.1
Norfolk State University	1935	PU-4+G	7,458	6,324	84.8	864	11.6
Saint Paul's College	1888	PR-4	736	711	96.6	16	2.2
The Virginia College	1888	PR-4	40	40	100.0	0	0.0
**Virginia State University	1882	PU-4+G	3,583	3,070	85.7	425	11.9
Virginia Union University	1865	PR-4+G	1,108	1,091	98.5	8	0.7

WEST VIRGINIA

West Virginia State College	1891	PU-4	4,029	517	12.8	3,464	86.0

*1986 racial/ethnic data are not available for 15 of the 104 historically black colleges and universities. Racial/ethnic data for these 15 institutions were imputed from the 1984 Office of Civil Rights *Racial, Ethnic and Sex Enrollment Data for Institutions of Higher Education* (Unpublished data). Analysis does not include unclassified students.

Note: Other historically black colleges not included in the analysis are: Bluefield State College, Bluefield, WV (founded in 1895 and presently a predominantly white institution), and Interdenominational Theological Center, Atlanta, GA (founded in 1958 and currently a viable institution).

**The 1890 Land Grant Institutions

***Legend: PU-4   — Public 4 Year
            PU-4+G   — Public 4 Year + Graduate
            PR-2   — Public 2 Year
            PR-4   — Private 4 Year
            PR-4+G   — Private 4 Year + Graduate
            PR-2   — Private 2 Year
            PR-4+GP — Private 4 Year + Graduate Professional
            PR-G   — Private Graduate Only

Source: NAFEO Annual Fall Enrollment Survey (1986) of Undergraduate, Graduate and Professional Students.

TABLE 2
A Summary
Historically Black Colleges and Universities by Control, Level and Date Established
NAFEO Membership (N = 104)

Date Established	Number	Control		Level					
		Public	Private	2-Year	4-Year	4-Year + Graduate	4-Year + Grad/Prof	Grad. and Professional	Graduate Only
1979–1987	1		1					1	
1964–1978	1	1		1					
1949–1963	6	5	1	3		3			
1924–1948	5	4	1	2		3			
1909–1923	4	2	2	1	1	2			
1894–1908	16	8	8	3	7	6			
1879–1893	25	10	15	4	14	5	2		
1864–1878	39	10	29	1	24	11	1	1	1
1849–1863	6	4	2		5	1			
1834–1848	1	1				1			
Total	104	45	59	15	51	32	3	2	1
Percent	100	43	57	14	49	31	3	2	1

Source: NAFEO Research Office

TABLE 3

Percent of Black and White Students Enrolled in Other NAFEO Equal Opportunity Educational Colleges and Universities, Fall, 1986

NAFEO Membership (N=12)

State/Institutions	Date Estab.	Control/*** Level	Total Students	Black Total	Black Percent	White Total	White Percent
CALIFORNIA							
Compton Community College	1927	PU-2	3,439	2,386	69.4	99	2.9
Charles R. Drew Postgraduate Medical School	1966	PR-GP	950	950	100.0	0	0.0
GEORGIA							
Atlanta Jr. College	1974	PU-2	1,281	1,160	90.6	29	2.3
ILLINOIS							
Chicago State University	1867	PU-4	7,762	6,460	83.2	951	12.3
Kennedy-King College	1935	PU-2	4,236	4,126	97.4	17	0.4
MARYLAND							
*Sojourner-Douglass College	1972	PR-4	383	380	99.2	2	0.5
MASSACHUSETTS							
*Roxbury Community College	1973	PU-2	1,187	540	45.5	271	22.8

21

TABLE 3 (Continued)

State/Institutions	Date Estab.	Control/*** Level	Total Students	Black Total	Black Percent	White Total	White Percent
MICHIGAN							
*Highland Park Community College	1918	PU-2	2,416	2,324	96.2	54	2.2
*Lewis College of Business	1929	PR-2	338	338	100.0	0	0.0
Wayne County Community College	1969	PU-2	10,528	6,364	60.4	3,444	32.7
NEW YORK							
Medgar Evers College	1969	PU-4	2,544	2,544	100.0	0	0.0
OHIO							
Cuyahoga Community College	1971	PU-2	23,655	5,916	25.0	16,715	70.6

*Data imputed from The Civil Rights *Racial, Ethnic and Sex Enrollment Survey for Higher Education* (unpublished date). Analysis does not include unclassified students.

***Legend:
PU-4 — Public 4 Year Institution
PU-4+G — Public 4 Year + Graduate Institution
PU-2 — Public 2 Year Institution
PR-4 — Private 4 Year Institution
PR-4+G — Private 4 Year + Graduate Institution
PR-2 — Private 2 Year Institution
PR-GP — Private Graduate and First Professional
PR-G — Private Graduate Only

Source: NAFEO Annual Fall Enrollment Survey (1986) of Undergraduate, Graduate and Professional Students.

TABLE 4
A Summary
Other NAFEO Equal Opportunity Educational Colleges and Universities by Control, Level and Date Established NAFEO Membership (N = 12)

Date Established	Number	Control		Level			
		Public	Private	2-Year	4-Year	4-Year + Graduate	Grad. and Professional
1979–1987							
1964–1978	7	5	2	4	2		1
1949–1963							
1924–1948	3	2	1	3			
1909–1923	1	1		1			
1894–1908							
1879–1893							
1864–1878	1	1				1	
1849–1863							
1834–1848							
Total	12	9	3	8	2	1	1
Percent	100	75	25	67	17	8	8

Source: NAFEO Research Office

23

TABLE 6

Historically and Predominantly Black Colleges Now Closed

(N = 14)

Institution	Location
Bulter Junior College	Tyler, TX
Daniel Payne College	Birmingham, AL
Durham College	Durham, NC
Friendship College	Rock Hill SC
J. P. Campbell College	Jackson, MS
Kittrell College	Kittrell, NC
Mary Allen Junior College	Crockett, TX
Mississippi Industrial College	Holly Spring, MS
Okolona College	Okolona, MS
Saints Junior College	Lexington, MS
Shaw College of Detroit	Detroit, MI
Storer College	Harper Ferry, WV
T. J. Harris Junior College	Meridan, MS
Piney Woods County Life School	Piney Woods, MS
(Now offering a nursery through	
12th grade program)	

Source: NAFEO Archives

statistical study that related the decline in black student enrollment at private colleges and universities to the lack of adequate student financial aid. In a running debate with the Administration, which has challenged the findings, NAICU has stoutly defended its research conclusions. The American Association of State Colleges and Universities (ASSCU) has surveyed its membership to identify exemplary programs for retaining minority students. The Association presented success stories of model minority retention programs at state colleges and universities at its annual meeting in the fall of 1987.

The *Chronicle of Higher Education* assigned a number of its editors to focus on different aspects of minorities in higher education and devoted a major part of its Fall, 1987 issue to this subject.

The State Higher Education Executive Officers and the Education Commission of the States have issued a series of publications describing minority participation in higher education and document that "progress is distressingly stalled." The organizations have jointly published reports on trends and state initiatives concerning minorities in higher education. The College Board has published a detailed analysis of minorities in higher education and graduate school. The School of Education of Harvard University under a grant from the Ford Foundation, has published in 1988 a volume, *Desegregating America's Colleges and Universities,* edited by John D. Williams, III, which presents papers by some of the nation's leading educators on various facets of the Title IV regulation of higher education. The rationale for commissioning the papers is to address "the issue of black American's limited access to higher education." The National Center for Postsecondary Governance and Finance at Arizona State University even more recently assembled educational leaders from throughout the country to consider a series of commissioned papers focusing on various facets of minority participation in postsecondary education. The Massachusetts Institute of Technology, funded by $1.2 Million grant by the Carnegie Corporation, has established a thirty-three member National Council to develop a blueprint for action for the education of minorities. The group has already held an invitational conference at which representatives from many national associations described their activities relative to studying or conducting action programs concerning minorities in postsecondary education. For the most part, this renewed interest in minorities in higher education is directed toward all minorities rather than blacks alone, and focuses primarily on blacks at predominantly white institutions. Current policies directed toward INTEGRATION may or may not have a favorable impact on the historically black colleges and the significant number of students they serve. NAFEO presidents have discussed this issue with the current Administration which has now undertaken a major study of minority access into postsecondary education.

President Reagan has consistently articulated his commitment to the historically black colleges and Universities (HBCUs) and over the years has periodically met with the historically black college presidents. In the spring of 1987, NAFEO representatives expressed their concern to President Reagan over the declining trends of black student enrollment in postsecondary education. They further expressed their concern that administration policies might be contributing to these declines, and, in contradiction with the Presidents Executive Order, having a deleterious effect on historically black colleges.

President Reagan directed that the Director of the Office of Management and Budget (OMB) meet with NAFEO presidents to discuss their concerns in greater detail. Two such meetings have been held to date. The NAFEO presidents reiterated their concern about the decline of black students in postsecondary education and the possibility that the Administration's shift of emphasis to loans from grants in student financial aid packages may have contributed to this decline. The OMB Director listened to the concerns of the presidents, discussed them thoroughly and promised to have his staff compile data to serve as a basis of giving an initial reaction.

The following staff report, based on data from the Current Population Survey, indicates, according to the

Administration, that the major slide in the college-going rate of black high school graduates preceded the accession of this Administration to office. Therefore, the Administration contended, it is erroneous to establish a cause and effect relationship between Administration policies and trend declines in this particular series.

• High school graduation rates for blacks ages 18–24 increased from 67.5 percent in 1976 to 75.5 percent in 1985.

• Of these high school graduates, 33.5 percent enrolled in colleges in 1976. This rate then dropped to 27.6 percent in 1980, and has remained relatively constant since that time. As of 1985, 26.1 percent of black high school graduates age 18–24 enrolled in postsecondary education.

• Of the total black 18–24 year old population (high school graduates and non-graduates), 22.6 percent enrolled in college in 1976, dropping to 19.2 percent in 1980, and then remaining relatively constant. The rate was 19.7 percent in 1985.

• These data do *not* include proprietary schools (private for-profit vocational schools) and so understate black participation in postsecondary education. There is evidence that black enrollment in such schools has increased sharply in recent years.

The NAFEO presidents hypothesized that the drop in enrollment was traceable to the fact that available student financial aid, when adjusted for inflation, has declined and that the shift of emphasis from grants to loans has adversely affected the enrollment of black students since low income persons are unfamiliar with banks, have a reluctance to borrow and would be discouraged from enrolling in college if they had to borrow to do so.

The Administration's response was that student financial aid has expanded dramatically even in constant dollars, that low income students have constituted an increasingly large percentage of the recipients and have gotten an increasingly larger share of the financial aid dollars. Finally, the response continues, there is no conclusive evidence that lower income students are reluctant to borrow.

Following is an extract from the Staff Report:

• The availability of Federal Title IV student aid has grown dramatically in recent years, from $8.9 billion in 1980 to $13.7 billion in 1986 (the last year for which actual data are available), an increase of 55 percent. The corresponding increase in the Consumer Price Index is 30 percent.

• Data on the racial distribution of Pell grants are not available. Using low income (each year's poverty level for a family of four) as a proxy, we find that both the share of recipients who are disadvantaged and the share of Pell funds going to these disadvantaged recipients have been increasing in recent years:

	Percent Below Poverty Line			
	1983–84	1984–85	1985–86	1986–87 (est.)
Share of recipients	51.3	59.9	63.4	70.3
Share of dollars	69.3	71.9	72.8	77.7

• There is also no conclusive evidence that the propensity to borrow decreases with income. A recent College Board study also found that available research does not provide evidence that actual or potential debt burden interferes with student decisions about postsecondary enrollment and completion.

On July 24, 1987, President Reagan issued a new memorandum reinforcing his commitment to Executive Order #12320 on strengthening the historically black colleges and directing heads of the twenty-seven agencies that provide the bulk of funding to historically black colleges "to make sure that agency officials understand the high priority that I personally place on this initiative." The President asked these top officials to involve the HBCUs in matters that would involve the agencies in fulfilling their own mission but that could concomitantly "lead to a permanent improvement in the quality of the HBCUs programs." In addition, the President asked agencies to identify "ways to forge long-term links between specific schools and the private sector." The President then directed the Secretary of Education to identify long-term and short-term strategies to address the issues of minority postsecondary enrollment. Following is an extract from President Reagan's memorandum:

I direct the Secretary of Education to contact a thorough study of the factors that affect minority postsecondary enrollment, both financial and nonfinancial, and provide the results to me and to the Director of the Office of Management and Budget no later than June 1, 1988. The study should be comprehensive in scope and should include any recommendations of the Secretary for cost-effective approaches to increasing minority enrollment.

The National Association for Equal Opportunity in Higher Education (NAFEO) will highlight the issues of minorities in higher education at its National Conference on Blacks in Higher Education in 1988. It will accord appropriate attention to issues on blacks in higher education and particularly the historically black colleges and universities (HBCUs). NAFEO will assemble reseachers from major associations conducting studies or developing policies concerning minorities in higher education to assure that the contractor conducting research for the department of education will have access to the most accurate and recent relevant data concerning all minorities including blacks and the historically black colleges. It is the expectation that the researcher having access to these data will be in a better position to provide sound policy recommendations to President Reagan by June, 1988.

Additional questions have been raised about the continued enhancement of the historically black colleges and universities (HBCUs) as integration in higher education proceeds. In December 1987, US District Court Judge John Pratt ruled in favor of the Office for Civil Rights (OCR) of the U.S. Department of Education, which had sought relief as the defendant in the Adams vs. Bennett case. Judge Pratt granted that relief. He indicated that in light of recent Supreme Court rulings, OCR could no longer be considered a defendant, because technically it did not cause the discrimination that Judge Pratt believes continued to exist. In addition, since the original plaintiffs were no longer students, plaintiffs no longer had legal standing. Judge Pratt seemed to keep the door open for new plaintiffs, possibly on the State level to file suit continued the desegregation process. The NAACP Legal Defense and Educational Fund has appealed Judge Pratt's ruling.

Plaintiffs in another desegregation case, Ayers vs. the State of Mississippi, also suffered a setback in December 1987. Judge Neal B. Biggers, Jr., of the U.S. District Court in the northern District of Mississippi finds a final judgment ruling that "the court finds no proof in this record of current violation of the constitution or statutes of the United States by the defendants. This case should, therefore, be dismissed." The court further stated that the problem was not that of failure on the part of defendants to fulfill their affirmative duty to desegregate higher education, rather legislature having limited financial resources seeking to fund too many institutions. This implicit suggestion of closing or merging institutions could pose a threat for one or more historically black colleges in Mississippi.

Soon after these court rulings, Secretary William Bennett of the U.S. Department of Education, held a press conference to announce that ten states had made "significant and substantial progress in desegregating their systems of public higher education." He announced that four states, Arkansas, North Carolina, South Carolina and West Virginia had acceptable desegregation plans and that OCR would take no additional steps to monitor these states. The Secretary indicated that six additional states, Delaware, Florida, Georgia, Missouri, Oklahoma and Virginia showed additional progress within ninety days, primarily in the area of enhancing historically black colleges and expanding the enrollment of minority students. These plans also would be acceptable. Shifts in public policy on integregation in higher education will become clearer as executive or judicial decisions respond to the desegregation plans of Kentucky, Maryland, Pennsylvania, and Texas or to results of litigation of Alabama, Louisiana, Mississippi and Ohio which challenged OCR directive to develop a plan.

References

Haynes, Leonard L. *A critical examination of the Adams case: A source book.* Washington, D.C.: Institute for Services to Education, 1978.

Hill, Susan. *The traditionally black institutions of higher education: 1860–1982.* Washington, D.C.: The National Center for Education Statistics, 1984.

U.S. Department of Commerce (Bureau of the Census). *National data book and guide to sources: Statistical abstract of the United States—1987,* 107th Edition, December, 1986.

The National Institute of Independent Colleges and Universities and the United Negro College Fund, Inc. *Access to college: The impact of federal financial and policies at private historically black colleges* by Julianne S. Thriff and Alan H. Kirschner, Washington, D.C., 1987.

NAFEO Research Institute. Analysis of DE/OCR data tapes on earned degrees conferred from institutions of higher education by race/ethnicity, and sex, academic years—1980–81, 1982–83, and 1984–85.

NAFEO Research Institute. Analysis of DE/OCR data tapes of fall enrollment—1980–81, 1982–83, and 1984–85.

National Advisory Committee. Analysis of OCR unpublished data of fall enrollment—1975–76, 1976–77, and 1978–79.

National Advisory Committee. Analysis of DE/OCR unpublished data on earned degrees—1975–76, 1976–77, and 1978–79.

United States Commission on Civil Rights. *The black/white colleges: dismantling the dual system of higher education,* Clearinghouse Publication 66, Washington, D.C., April, 1981.

U.S. Department of Education, Center for Statistics—OERI. *Digest of education statistics: 1985–86,* Washington, D.C., February, 1986.

Gillespi, D. A. & Carlson, N. *Trends in student aid: 1983 to 1986,* Washington, D.C.: The College Board, 1987.

Hansen, J. S. *Student loans: Are they overburdening a generation?* Washington, D.C., Joint Economic Committee, December, 1986.

Fleming, Jacqueline. *Blacks in college,* San Francisco: Jossey-Bass Publications, 1985.

Astin, Alexander W. *Minorities in American higher education: Recent trends, current prospects, and recommendations.* San Francisco: Jossey-Bass Publications, 1985.

National Research Council. *Summary report 1984: Doctorate recipients from United States universities* (Susan L. Coyle, editor). Washington, D.C.: National Academy Press, 1986.

32

Chapter 2
Strategies for Combating Racism and Implementing Goals To Achieve Equity for Blacks in Higher Education

Dr. Julia E. Wells
Coordinator, South Carolina Higher
Education Desegregation Plan

Racism stems from the belief that a person's racial designation or ethnic origin causes intellectual or moral inferiority. The alleged inferiority of Afro-Americans is a racist belief that has persisted throughout America's history. That Afro-Americans are inferior has been argued by Thomas Jefferson and a host of pro-slavery advocates, by white supremacists during and after Reconstruction, and by "scientific" racists in the twentieth century. Equality for Afro-Americans, in turn, has been defended by Quakers, abolitionists, and black leaders such as Benjamin Banneker, Frederick Douglass, Malcolm X, and Martin Luther King. Other defenders include social scientists W.E.B. Dubois, Gunnar Myrdal, Kenneth Clark, and numerous others. When racist beliefs by individuals (individual racism) translate to racist behavior, harmful injustices are rendered against blacks. When racist beliefs are incorporated into the system that constitute the infrastructure of our society (institutional/systemic racism), the resulting institutional or systemic racism is harmful not only to the blacks who are targets, but also erodes the core of idealism and progress in American society. Racism is like a cancer that destroys the American dream for the blacks who become its victims.

In this country, institutional racism has victimized Afro-Americans through (1) the institution of chattel slavery, (2) the "legal" segregation of races, and (3) the discriminatory Jim Crow practices and customs. Furthermore, racially discriminatory practices are too frequently found in the criminal justice system and in hiring and promotions in the workplace. Racial "incidents" and racial harassment of blacks continue to occur with seemingly increasing frequency in the 1980s. It is obvious that racism is harmful to Afro-Americans; is harmful to America; it is wrong.

Federally Mandated Desegregation Plans:
An Idealistic Approach to Achieve Equity for Blacks in
Certain Higher Education Systems

Historically, Afro-Americans have been idealists and devotees of the American dream of equality and freedom. Accordingly, in 1970, The National Association for

34

the Advancement of Colored People (NAACP) brought suit to compel enforcement of Title VI cases, including public systems of higher education, alleging inadequate enforcement by the Office for Civil Rights (OCR). The Adams case was filed in October, 1970, by the NAACP as a class action suit in the U.S. District Court for the District of Columbia with Judge John H. Pratt, presiding. The suit was filed on behalf of two groups of plaintiffs: (1) students attending schools and colleges that had, since the "enactment of the Civil Rights Act of 1964, segregated and discriminated on the basis of race in violation of the fourteenth amendment . . . and yet continued to receive federal financial assistance, contrary to Title VI of the 1964 Civil Rights Act," and (2) citizens and federal taxpayers whose taxes were being expended by the defendant through grants to public schools and colleges that segregated and discriminated on the basis of race.

Named as defendants in the suit were Elliot T. Richardson, then Secretary of the Department of Health, Education and Welfare (HEW) and Stanley Pottinger, Director of the OCR. These men were cited because at that time, they exercised HEW's responsibility for enforcement of Title VI. Kenneth R. Adams, a student from Brandon, Mississippi, was first on the alphabetical list of plaintiffs listed in the suit. Hence, the legal title of the case was first known as *Adams vs. Richardson*.

By 1981, more than a dozen states that formerly operated segregated dual systems of higher education were cited for violating Title VI of the Civil Rights Act of 1964. Four states (Louisiana, Mississippi, Ohio, and Alabama) were referred to the Department of Justice, and 14 states negotiated plans with the OCR to remedy the violation of Title VI by making commitments to remove the vestiges of *de jure* segregation through a wide variety of activities. These states were: Arkansas, Delaware, Florida, Georgia, Kentucky, Maryland, Missouri, North Carolina, Oklahoma, Pennsylvania, South Carolina, Texas, Virginia, West Virginia.

Each state's desegregation plan was supposed to have been tailored to the unique situation in the state (size and mission of each institution, geographic location and number and percentage of black residents). All of the plans focused on three broad areas of desegregation:

1. disestablishment of the structure of the dual system (primarily enhancement of traditionally black institutions);

2. desegregation of student enrollment; and

3. desegregation of faculty, administrative staffs, non-academic personnel and governing boards.

Ten of the 14 states have plans that expired during the 1985–86 year.

Evidence of Racism
(Vestiges of Segregation) in Higher Education

Despite the efforts of states and institutions to remove vestiges of segregation as mandated in the various desegregation plans, a number of trends and conditions in higher education provide evidence that racism in America continues to negatively influence black racial progress. In 1987, we are experiencing

• declines in black undergraduate enrollment;

36

- declines in the number and proportion of blacks earning bachelors, masters, and doctorate degree;
- declines in the number and percent of black faculty and executive staff at colleges and universities;
- declines in amount of scholarships and financial aid awarded (and available) to black students; and
- increasingly frequent incidents of racial incidents and harassment of black students attending traditionally white campuses.

Strategies for Combating Racism in Higher Education

The following strategies are recommended for reducing and/or eradicating racism in higher education:

1. *First of all, we must never accept the notion that Afro-Americans are inferior.* The greatest obstacle to overcome race prejudice would be the acceptance by blacks of second class or inferior status. We must continue to believe in the concept of equality as an ideological bulwark against the pervasive and persistent assertion by some that Afro-Americans are stupid and, therefore, do not deserve to be treated equally. We must continue to insist that second best is not good enough. We must never "adjust" to racism or permit black youth to benignly tolerate racist treatment. We must maintain a strong sense of who we are and convey this self-esteem to black college students as well.

2. *Secondly, we should identify those activities that*

were effective in achieving desegregation goals and take necessary steps to insure that these activities are "institutionalized," that is, continued as on-going parts of college and university operations, even if federal pressures to desegregate are discontinued. States and institutions are obligated to insure equal access, equal treatment and equal outcomes for students in a nondiscriminatory manner. Effective recruitment and retention strategies for insuring access for black students are essential now and in the future, if declining black student enrollment is to be reversed.

3. *Efforts to add more black faculty and administrators must be continued.* Affirmative action goals should continue to be established and met by colleges and universities. Further, affirmative steps should be taken to support larger numbers of black students to earn graduate degrees that will qualify them to teach at the college/university level.

4. *A financial aid crisis for poor black students should not be permitted to continue.* Steps should be taken to make essential aid available to students who need such aid in order to begin or continue their college studies. Declines in available federal student aid make it essential for other sources of aid (state, corporate, church, other, etc.) to be identified and made available to black students.

5. *Activities and projects that were implemented in higher education institutions in the "Adams" states to remove vestiges of segregation should be described, evaluated, and disseminated.* Summaries of the descriptions and evaluations should be made

available to other institutions and states so that successful projects, activities and/or strategies may be replicated as may be appropriate.

6. *Federal and state governments should encourage and provide support for research projects that address educational problems affecting black racial progress in America.* The results of such research might be expected to provide models for coping with the new forms of racism (on-campus racial "incidents," workplace racial harassment, deprivation of economic advantages based on race, etc.) that face this generation of Americans.

7. *Finally, we must establish effective networks and mentoring relationships among ourselves and others to insure that the idealism envisioned in the concept of black racial equality will prevail, and indeed, be implemented to the highest extent possible by us and by future generations.*

This article is an abstract of a paper presented by Dr. Julia E. Wells, Coordinator of the South Carolina Higher Education Desegregation Plan, at the NAFEO 12th National Conference on Blacks in Higher Education on April 9–12, 1987.

Bibliography

Haynes, Leonard L. *A critical examination of the Adams case: A source book.* Washington, D.C.: Institute for Services to Education, 1978.

S. C. Commission on Higher Education. *Final comprehensive report on implementation of the S. C. plan for equity and equal opportu-*

nity in the public colleges and universities. Columbia, S. C., March 31, 1986.

U. S. Department of Education. *Proposed factual report on South Carolina's higher education desegregation plan.* Washington, D. C., March 27, 1987.

Chapter 3
Desegregation Activities at Maryland's Historically Black Public Institutions for Undergraduate Higher Education
"An Abstract"

Dr. Paul L. Fairley
Acting Director
Analysis and Data Collection Services
Office of Civil Rights, the Department
of Education

This study critically reviewed steps taken by Maryland to enhance and desegregate its public black colleges with limited knowledge of the adequacy of its enhancement effort or the comparative effectiveness of "desegregation" activities. Through structured interviews at the four historically black colleges and universities in Maryland (Bowie State College, Coppin State College, Morgan State University, and the University of Maryland-Eastern Shore Campus), this study obtained from 39 black college administrators their perception of the adequacy of enhancement resource estimates and assessments of the effectiveness of component "desegregation" activities. Additionally, it sought to determine if these measures differed significantly on the basis of whether the administrators functioned as executive level administrative staff (ELAS) or mid-level administrative staff (MLAS).

Specifically, the following two research questions were addressed:

Research Question 1. How do administrators of the historically black colleges view the adequacy of fiscal resource estimates determined and required by the State Board in addressing previously identified deficiencies of the historically black colleges? Put differently, do they regard the resource estimates as being adequate to enhance their comparability to traditionally white institutions with the same, or similar, educational missions?

Research Question 2. How do the administrators of the historically black colleges assess the effectiveness of the programs and activities funded under "desegregation" in terms of achieving increases in the enrollment of full-time undergraduate other-race students at these institutions?

Dr. Fairley gives background information pertaining to desegregation activities in higher education, specifically focusing on Maryland higher education. In *Adams V. Richardson* (1973) the court found that ten southern and border states were violating the requirements of the Civil Rights Act of 1964 by continuing to maintain vestiges of segregated systems of higher education. Maryland was one of the violating states.

In reaction to the heightened federal enforcement activity and faced with the possibility of federal funding termination, a *Maryland Plan For Completing the Desegregation of the Public Post-secondary Education Institutions in the State* (the 1974 state plan) was developed by the state's executive branch and submitted to the federal government. The 1974 state plan set 1980 projections for racial composition of the state's four public black colleges and proposed a series of programs and activities which were expected to have as their end result the desegregation of the public black colleges (see Tables 1 and 2).

Dr. Fairley goes on to state that by 1985 the legal stalemates between OCR and Maryland brought on by

TABLE 1
The 1974 Racial Composition and 1980 Enrollment Goals for Maryland's Public Historically Black Institutions

Institution	1974 State Plan 1980 Goal— Percent Black Full-Time Undergraduates	1980 State Plan 1985 Goal— Percent Black Full-Time, First-Time Freshmen
Bowie	51–52	71
Coppin	73–80	95
Morgan	73–77	88
Univ. of Maryland (Eastern Shore)	50–60	75

Source: The Maryland Council for Higher Education Report, 1974, pp. 11–17. Maryland State Board for Higher Education, *Enhancement of Maryland's Predominantly Black Collegiate Institutions,* Annapolis, MD, 1980, p. 49.

TABLE 2

Achievement of Racial Composition Projections For Maryland's Public Historically Black Institutions

Institution	1975		1980		1980 Goals
	Total	% Black	Total	% Black	% Black
Bowie	1,649	80.9	1,292	83.2	51–52
Coppin	2,044	87.7	1,832	94.0	73–80
Morgan	4,190	89.9	3,722	91.6	73–77
Univ. of Maryland (Eastern Shore)	871	74.1	831	78.2	50–60

Source: Maryland State Board for Higher Education, *Seventh Annual Desegregation Report in Maryland's Public Postsecondary Educational Institutions, 1974–1980*, p. 16.

the temporary injunction granted by Judge Northrop of the U.S. District Court of Maryland on March 9, 1976, in *Mandel v. HEW* had remained in effect for nine years. Judge Northrop then brought pressure to bear upon the parties to negotiate resolution of the conflict. On June 28, 1985, Governor Harry Hughes submitted to OCR Maryland's *Plan to Ensure Equal Post-Secondary Educational Opportunity: 1985–1990* (the 1985 state plan). A principal objective of the 1985 state plan was the

> . . . enhancement of Maryland's traditional black institutions to ensure that they are comparable and competitive with the traditionally white institutions with respect to capital facilities, operating budgets, and new academic programs. (p.4)

To achieve this end, Maryland made a commitment to allocate to the public black colleges $11.7 million over and above normal operating budget levels and $64.7 million in projected capital expenditures. In terms of changes in racial enrollment goals for the public black colleges as described in Table 2, the 1985 state plan anticipates black enrollments in 1989 as follows: Bowie—71% (no change); Coppin—85% (-10%); Morgan—85% (-3%); and UMES—75% (no change).

Although the 1985 state plan described in detail the methodology employed in developing the racial enrollment goals for blacks attending traditionally white institutions, no such discussion is provided to support the derivation of other-race enrollment goals for the black colleges. Additionally, the plan provides no discussion of desegregation programs and activities to be undertaken at the black colleges so as to achieve the 1989 other-race enrollment goals.

Nevertheless, OCR confirmed that the 1985 state plan provisions conformed with the requirements of Title VI (CRA). As a result of the OCR/Maryland agreement and the U.S. District Court of Maryland's entry of a companion consent decree executed by the parties, the legal stalemate of *Mandel V. HEW* has ostensibly ended.

In addition, in 1985, the Maryland General Assembly authorized the governor to establish a Governor's Commission on Excellence in Higher Education to examine and report to the governor concerning the status of funding and the quality of higher education in the state. In October 1985 the Governor announced the membership of the Commission.

Findings of the Study

The administrators perceived the fiscal estimates determined by the state as needed to enhance the black colleges to comparability with traditionally white colleges as less than adequate. Providing financial grants to other-race students (ORGP) was considered as the most effective "desegregation" activity, with recruitment next most effective, and other-race personnel for services to other-race students least effective. Significant ELAS/MLAS differences were (1) MLAS appeared to assess recruitment as more effective and "desegregation" expenditures as more adequate than ELAS and (2) ELAS appeared to assess ORGP (other-race grants) as more effective than MLAS.

Maryland has undertaken substantive actions to enhance its public black colleges, but more needs to be done. While ORGP was considered the most effective "desegregation" activity, the study suggested that expenditures for "desegregation" have been less than adequate to achieve undergraduate racial enrollment proportions that would suggest that these are no longer segregated institutions. The author did not seek to draw rigid conclusions on significant differences in responses of the ELAS and MLAS on certain interview items because of the research methodology employed.

The study offers recommendations to various state agencies, the Maryland General Assembly, and the federal government for policy analyses, programmatic and administrative actions, and further research which, it is believed, will be helpful to the state's efforts to eliminate vestiges of a dual higher education system.

1. A second enhancement study of the black colleges should be undertaken so that findings with fiscal resource requirement estimates can be incorporated into the 1990 state plan which will be developed and submitted to OCR. The study should also examine and identify resources needed to bring the

black colleges' auxiliary enterprise facilities, programs, and activities into comparability. A task force to accomplish this study should be appointed by the Maryland State Board for Higher Education (SBHE).

2. The SBHE should exclude and identify separately enhancement costs from the budget process formulae used to make interinstitutional comparisons and set institutional comparisons and set institutional allocations. These are legal costs and represent catch-up costs needed to overcome past inequalities. The SBHE, to test the issue of social costs, should put in place a longitudinal study that analyzes the cost effectiveness of state support for remedial activities related to the enrollment in the black colleges of educationally disadvantaged black high school graduates as against the social costs related to state costs associated with nonpostsecondary enrollment of educationally disadvantaged black high school graduates.

3. State policy which requires financial need as the basis for awarding other-race grants at the public black colleges should be eliminated.

4. The SBHE should develop a methodology for determining other-race enrollment goals for the public black colleges for inclusion in the 1990 state plan. The black colleges should be integrally involved in the development of the methodology.

5. Separate studies of black colleges should be pursued to determine the existence of attitudinal barriers to increasing other-race enrollment, the magnitude of such barriers should they exist, and the

development of recommendations to overcome such barriers.

6. Added priority should be given by the SBHE to the establishment and placement of new academic programs at the historically black colleges. In an effort to minimize and eliminate duplication of programs at historically black and traditionally white colleges, black colleges should be afforded more priority in program continuations.

7. Given the declining enrollment rates experienced by the public black colleges in recent years which some interpret as being related to desegregation, the Maryland General Assembly should consider relaxation of policies which have had the effect of limiting the enrollment of out-of-state students at the public black colleges pending achievement of enhancement goals to which the state has committed.

8. The U.S. District Court for the District of Columbia and the Legal Defense Fund should review the 1985 state plan for consistency with *Adams* requirements.

9. The generalizability of the study's findings should be determined by other states affected by *Adams*, since many of these states offer desegregation programs and activities similar to Maryland and are facing difficulty in increasing other-race enrollment at their public historically black colleges. Separate studies should be undertaken to determine the adequacy of enhancement efforts and the effectiveness of desegregation programs aimed at increasing other-race enrollment in such states.

Source: Fairley, Paul L. *Desegregation Activities at Maryland's Historically Black Public Institutions for Undergraduate Education.* Unpublished doctoral dissertation, University of Miami, 1986.

References

Adams v. Califano, 430 F. Supp. 118 (D.D.C. 1977).

Adams v. Richardson, 356 F. Supp. 92, 94 (D.D.C., 1973).

Adams v. Richardson, F.2d 1159, 1164–65 (D.D.C. Cir. 1973).

Adams v. Weinberger, 391 F. Supp. 269 (D.D.C. 1975).

Appleton, N. (1983). *Cultural pluralism in education.* New York: Longman.

Blake, E. (1976). *Public policy and the higher education of black Americans.* Staff report of the Subcommittee on Constitutional Rights, Committee on the Judiciary. 94th Congress, Second Session.

Blouner, R. (1972). *Racial oppression in America.* New York: Harper & Row.

Bowie State College. (1981). U.S. Department of Education grant No. 031BZ0098 providing an institutional development grant.

Boules, F. & DeCosta, F. (1971). *Between two worlds: A profile of Negro education.* New York: McGraw Hill.

Brazziel, W. F. (1983). Baccalaureate college of origin of black doctorate recipients. *The Journal of Negro Education, 52*(2).

Briggs v. Elliott, 98 F. Supp. 529 (E.D.S.C. 1951).

Brown, T. (1983, October). The integration gap. *Tony Brown's Journal,* p. 4.

Brown v. Board of Education of Topeka, 347 U.S. 483 (1954).

Brown v. Board of Education, 349 U.S. 294, 301 (1955).

Carmichael, S. & Hamilton, C. J. (1967). *Black Power.* New York: Random House.

Carnegie Commission on Higher Education. (1977). *From isolation to mainstream: Problems of the colleges funded for Negroes.* San Francisco, CA: Josey-Bass.

Civil Righrs Act of July 2, 1964, P.L. 88–352, Title VI, 601 Stat. 252 (1976) and Supp. II, 1978).

Davis v. County School Board of Prince Edward County, 103 F. Supp. 337 (E.D. VA, 1952).

de Tocqueville, A. (1960). *Democracy in America.* New York: Vintage.

Florida ex. rel. Hawkins v. Board of Control, 350 U.S. 413 (1956).

Frazier, E. (1957). *The Negro in the United States.* New York: McMillan Co.

Frieson, F. A. (1979). *A study of the political dynamics within and between the Maryland System of Higher Education and its four public black colleges.* Cornell, NY: Cornell University.

Gebhart v. Belton, 87 A.2d 862 (Del. ch. 1952).

Gibran, K. (1923). *The prophet.* New York: Knopf.

Hall, R. L. (1977). *Black separatism and social reality: Rhetoric and reason.* New York: Pergaman.

Hall, R. L. (1978). *Black separatism in the United States.* Hanover, NH: University Press of New England.

Hall, R. L. (1979). *Ethnic autonomy—comparative dynamics: The Americas, Europe, and the developing world.* New York: Pergaman.

Higher Education Research Institute. (1982). *Final report of the commission on the higher education of minorities.* San Francisco, CA: Jossey-Bass.

Hollander, Sidney and Associates. A study of racial integration in the Maryland state colleges. Baltimore, MD: Maryland Council for Higher Education.

Howard University. (1978). *More power than progress.* Institute for the Study of Educational Policy. Washington, D.C.: Howard University.

Jones, T. J. (1916). *Negro education: A study of private and higher schools for colored people in the United States.* Washington, D.C.: U.S. Department of Interior, Bureau of Education. Vol. I.

Kallen, Horace M. (1924). *Culture and democracy in the United States.* New York: Liveright.

Katz, D. & Festinger, L. (1953). *Research methods in the behavioral sciences.* New York: Holt, Rhinehart & Winston.

50

Keys, J. (1977). *A survey of student personnel services in member colleges of the United Negro College Fund*. University of Miami, Coral Gables, FL.

Kerlinger, F. N. (1973). *Foundations of behavioral research*. New York: Holt, Rinehart & Winston.

Klein, A. J. (1930). *Survey of land-grant colleges and universities*. Washington, D.C.: U.S. Department of Interior, Bureau of Education. Vol. II.

Kluger, R. (1976). *Simple justice*. New York: Knopf.

Mandel v. HEW, 562 F.2d 914, 925–26 (4th Cir. 1977).

Maryland State Board for Higher Education. Internal staff paper, Discussion of capital and operating enhancement request. Annapolis, MD. Undated (1983).

Maryland State Board for Higher Education. (1981). *Enhancement of Maryland's predominantly black collegiate institutions*. Annapolis, MD.

Maryland State Board for Higher Education. (1982). *Fiscal year 1984 SBHE consolidated capital and operating budget for higher education*. Annapolis, MD.

Maryland State Board for Higher Education. (1983). *Fiscal year 1985, SBHE consolidated capital and operating budget for higher education*. Annapolis, MD.

Maryland State Board for Higher Education. (1982). *Maryland State Budget*. Vol. III.

Maryland State Board for Higher Education. (1974). *Plan for completing the desegregation of the public post-secondary education institutions in the state*.

Maryland State Board for Higher Education. (1985). *Plan to assure equal postsecondary educational opportunity*. Annapolis, MD.

Maryland State Board for Higher Education. (1982). *Seventh annual desegregation in Maryland's public postsecondary educational institutions: 1974–1980*.

McLaurin v. Oklahoma State Regents, 339 U.S. 637 (1950).

Missouri ex rel. Gaines v. Canada, 305 U.S. 337, 351 (1938).

Morrill Act of 1890, 7 U.S.C. Sec. 323 (1976).

National Advisory Committee on Black Higher Education and Black Colleges and Universities. *A losing battle: The decline in black participation in graduate and professional education.* Washington, D.C.: U.S. Government Printing Office.

Newman, W. M. (1973). *American pluralism: A study of minority groups and social theory.* New York: Harper & Row.

Norvelle, Merritt. (1976). *The desegregation of higher education: A case study of the problems and issues confronting the implementation of the Maryland Plan for completing the desegregation of its public post-secondary education institutions.* The University of Wisconsin: Madison, WI.

Pearson v. Murray, 182 A. 590. (Maryland, 1936).

Peterson, M. W. et al. (1978). *Black students on white campuses: The impact of increased black enrollments.* Ann Arbor, MI: University of Michigan.

Plessy v. Ferguson, 163 U.S. 537 (1896).

Preer, J. L. (1982). *Lawyers v. educators: black colleges and desegregation in public higher education.* Westport, CT: Greenwood.

Report of the National Advisory Commission on Civil Disorders. New York: Dutton.

Schuman, H. & Hatchett, S. (1974). *Black racial attitudes: Trends and complexities.* Ann Arbor: University of Michigan.

Selltiz, C. et al. (1959). *Research methods in social relations.* New York: Holt, Rhinehart & Winston.

Sipuel v. Board of Regents 332 U.S. 631, 632–33 (1948).

Sizemore, B. (1969). Separatism: A reality approach to inclusion. In *Racial Crisis in American education.* Chicago: Follet.

Southern Regional Education Board. Educational factors related to federal criteria for the desegregation of public postsecondary education. Atlanta, GA: 1980.

Southern Regional Education Board. Preliminary proposal to the U.S. Department of Education fund for the improvement of postsecondary education. Atlanta, GA: 1983.

Sweatt v. Painter, 339 U.S. 629, 635–36 (1950).

Thomas, S. (1984). *A social conflict theory analysis of the perceived effects of desegregation on blacks in higher education.* University of Miami: Coral Gables, FL.

U.S. Commission on Civil Rights. (1960). *Equal protection of the laws in higher education.* Washington, D.C.: Government Printing Office.

U.S. Commission on Civil Rights. (1981). *The black/white colleges: Dismantling the dual system of higher education.* Washington, D.C.: Government Printing Office.

U.S. Department of Education. (1983). *Annual federal plan of assistance to historically black colleges and universities in fiscal year 1983.* Washington, D.C.

U.S. Department of Education. (1982). *Final report to the Secretary on the annual federal plan to assist historically black colleges and universities in fiscal years 1981 and 1982.* Washington, D.C.

U.S. Department of Education. (1982). National Advisory Committee on Black Higher Education and Black Colleges and Universities. *Higher education equity: The crisis of appearance versus reality— revisited.* Washington, D.C.: Government Printing Office.

U.S. Department of Health, Education, and Welfare. (1978). *Criteria specifying the ingredients of acceptable plans to desegregate state systems of higher education.* 43 Fed. Reg. 6658–64.

U.S. Department of Health, Education, and Welfare. (1976). *Earned degrees survey.* National Center for Education Statistics. Washington, D.C.

U.S. Department of Health, Education, and Welfare. (1979). *Traditionally black institutions: A profile and an institutional directory.* National Center for Education Statistics. Washington, D.C.

U.S. Department of the Interior. (1928). *Survey of Negro colleges and universities.* Office of Education. Vol. 7. Washington, D.C.: Government Printing Office.

Wacker, R. (1983). *Ethnicity, pluralism and race.* Westport, CT: Greenwood Press.

Waters, L. A. (1981). *Evaluation of other race grant programs for graduate and professional school students.* Oct. 16, 1981, memorandum to Dr. Joseph Durham, Maryland State Board for Higher Education.

Weinberg, M. (1970). *Desegregation research: An appraisal.* Bloomington, IN: Phi Delta Kappa.

Williams. F. (1979). *Reasoning with statistics.* New York: Holt, Rhinehart & Winston.

Chapter 4

Black Faculty Recruitment and Retention: A Case Study

Dr. Louise Tomlinson
Assistant Professor
University of Georgia

In a 1975 survey of 131 institutions, the Carnegie Commission indicated that all respondents had devised an affirmative action plan but, of all submitted to the Office of Civil Rights, only 16 percent had been approved (Henry, 1980). Henry reported that "statistics do indicate a disproportionate representation of the "protected classes" [in] academic enterprise." The 1983–84 Annual Report of the Middle States Association for Colleges and Schools (MSACS) states that a national commitment to protect and promote the rights and opportunities of minorities has clearly diminished." Moreover, "the colleges and universities have followed this trend."

Status of Black Faculty Recruitment and Retention

To date, more than two decades since Title VII of the Civil Rights Act was amended to enforce compliance with Affirmative Action and Equal Employment, there has been only minimal progress toward proportionate representation of minorities, particularly black Americans, among the faculty ranks of institutions of higher education. According to Weinstein (1984), Associate Director of the Commission of Higher Education (CHE), "we have all been aware that those responsible for hiring of faculty and staff, particularly faculty search committees, would likely drag their feet in the hiring of women and minority people."

Although such discrimination has been taken as no surprise to some, what is even more alarming is a "solution" for the "problem" proposed by Hellweg and Churchman (1979) at an Association for Institutional Research Forum. The problem: "the continuing pressures that academic institutions are under to increase the number of women and minorities on their teaching staffs." The solution: "the use of adjunct faculty positions created with grant money to increase the numbers of women and minority faculty members." The explanation: "tenured faculty released to do research can be replaced through grant money by adjunct faculty selected to broaden the range of ideas and courses offered."

This justification sheds light on what has become not only a civil rights problem of discrimination evidenced by disproportionate representation of minorities in higher education, but also the disproportionate number of low-status faculty positions for which minorities are hired. In sum, the issue of minority faculty hiring is two-pronged: 1) there are not enough minority faculty being hired (particularly black Americans) and, 2) when they are hired, tenure, permanency and full-time status are scarce among their ranks.

The nature and scope of the problem have been documented from national, regional, and local perspectives, and among specific disciplines. From a regional perspective, Commission on Higher Education/Middle States Association of Colleges and Schools (CHE/MSACS) Associate Director Howard Simmons says of institutions in the middle states:

There is a lack of commitment to equity in the recruitment of minority students and the employment of minority faculty and staff in a large percentage of institutions visited. . . . More attention is being given to legalistic affirmative action and bureaucratic paperwork than to real enrollment and employment equity for blacks and Hispanics (1984, p. 2).

In a report to the National Association for Equal Opportunity in Higher Education, Nickson (1982) also addresses the absence of black faculty found by the National Urban League's Tri-State Minority Faculty Project. According to Nickson:

One fact became apparent. . . . If we wanted a true picture of the black professional presence within these institutions, we had to look beyond faculty positions to have any meaningful numbers to analyze, and/or discuss (p.1).

Reports on particular locales provide more details illustrating the inequity. For example, Nickson (1982) identifies the State University of New York (SUNY) as the largest majority university system in the world, having 64 campuses and a staff of over 27 thousand employees. According to Nickson, "a recent SUNY-wide review of only our state-operated campuses showed that of approximately 9 thousand faculty, 759 are minorities . . . 262 blacks, 114 Hispanics, and 376 Asians/Pacific Islanders, with 7 others."

The Staff Report of the Kentucky Commission on Human Rights indicates that at state colleges and universities the percentage and number of black faculty declined between 1979 and 1981. "Only 2.8 percent of faculty across the state were black in 1981" and "the number and percentage of black faculty new hires in the state supported-university system was lower in 1981 than in either 1977 or 1979, with blacks accounting for 13 of 382 (3.4%) new hires in 1981." In addition, community colleges continue to add black faculty within the system such that "none of the other seven white universities have come close in equalling the progress made by community colleges."

To determine why blacks are underrepresented in the field of nursing, the Program of Health Services Delivery, Bureau of Governmental Research, at the University of Maryland engaged in a three-year nationwide study including 40 schools in 16 states. The actual faculty racial composition was said to be closely aligned with the racial composition of questionnaire respondents in integrated schools, 81.0 percent white, 13.7 percent black. This can be interpreted as an abysmally disproportionate representation since all of the schools surveyed are "located within a major metropolitan area with large concentrations of black residents" in New York, North Carolina, Florida, Louisianna, and Illinois.

In the state of Georgia, the University System of Georgia Higher Education Staff Information EEO-6 report for 1985 indicates that, of all full-time tenured faculty, only 9.4 percent were black; and, of all other full-time faculty, only 6.2 percent were black. (It should be noted that, in each instance, individuals at the traditionally black institutions comprise 50 percent or more of all black faculty. There are only three traditionally black institutions within the system total of 34 institutions. Thus, percentages of full-time black faculty at the remaining institutions are critically lower than the system total indicates.) The 1985 report further indicates that of all part-time or temporary faculty 18.8 percent were black. Again, the data reveal disproportionate representation of blacks among faculty ranks and a greater percentage of non-tenure, temporary, and part-time status among the existing black faculty.

The literature indicates that there have been a great variety of efforts to improve minority faculty recruitment and hiring practices. However, this documentation does not reveal much information from the collective bodies of administrators within various systems of higher education in terms of their perceptions and suggestions in relation to the issues.

In addition to demographic studies of black faculty in systems of higher education, there is also a need for data which capture the perceptions, opinions and suggestions of administrators as they relate to faculty recruitment and retention. These data should do much to enhance the body of information from which future decisions are made for developing strategies for more effective affirmative action, equal opportunity, and all other related efforts.

The Study

The issues which are characteristic of the recruitment process for black faculty and the status of existing black faculty within systems of higher education are of a complex nature. However, the majority of these problems can be identified at the administrative levels of the system, since it is the administrative body which creates policy, makes leadership decisions, and sets the tone for the agenda of the academic community. A system-wide examination of the perceptions, opinions and suggestions of key administrators in relation to the recruitment and retention of black faculty should provide insight to the specific problems and possible solutions that exist for administrators in higher education. This study will focus on the issues, from an administrative perspective, in terms of roles, powers, responsibilities, leadership styles, planning, decision making and change.

Although consistent documentation of a quantitative nature exists (in Equal Opportunity Commission Surveys and other reports) to provide data on the numbers of minority faculty within systems of public higher education, there has been no comprehensive system-wide documentation of the qualitative aspects of the administrative processes involved in the hiring of such faculty. Existing documentation does not provide a means of understanding the individuals involved in the faculty hiring process in terms of their perceptions, opinions and suggestions as administrators.

The purpose of this study was to examine and describe the meanings which administrators ascribe to the social process of minority faculty recruitment and retention, by means of their stated perceptions, opinions and suggestions. More specifically, the intention of the study was to examine administrators' responses to the issues of recruiting and retaining black American faculty.

The data collection was conducted in two phases. First, a survey of six key administrators at each of 34 institutions in a system of public higher education was conducted by mail-out questionnaire. Second, on-site interviews were conducted with administrators at six of the institutions. The questionnaire and interview schedule were designed to parallel the Buckley and Feldbaum's (1979) instrument administered to guage faculty attitudinal and activity indicators related to the recruitment and retention of black students (Program of Health Services Delivery, Bureau of Governmental Research).

The questionnaire for this study was structured to guage administrative attitudinal and activity indicators related to the recruitment and retention of black faculty. In order to determine which factors are considered most critical to the issues of black faculty hiring practices, the questionnaire focused on: the recruitment process, search committees, impact of minority faculty, faculty assignments, professional status and promotion, recruitment and retention incentives, as well as general campus climate and other environmental factors. The instrument included addressing the categories described.

The survey was forwarded to the following key administrators at each institution in the system: the President, the Vice President for Academic Affairs (or Dean of the College), the Affirmative Action Officer, the Dean of the School of Business/Management (or Department Chair), the Dean of the School of Arts and Sciences/Humanities (or Department Chair), and the Dean of the School of Education where applicable. Participants were requested to complete all items of the questionnaire independent of any form of collaboration and to indicate where items

61

were not applicable by providing a brief explanation. Individuals were informed that all information provided would be treated confidentially and anonymously.

The on-site interviews were conducted with the same key administrators at three institutions identified as having a high percentage of black faculty, as compared to other institutions in the system—excluding the traditionally black, and, at three institutions identified as having comparatively low percentage of black faculty. Participants were again assured of confidentiality and anonymity.

Of a total of 168 questionnaires forwarded, 135 were received (an 80% response rate) and 122 were used for data analyses. (Responses from administrators at traditionally black institutions were eliminated from the sample with the realization that these responses could create results spurious to the intended focus on black faculty as a minority.)

Table I presents the demographic frequencies of the respondents. Of the 122 respondents in the sample, 21 percent were "currently" Presidents; 21 percent, Vice Presidents of Academic Affairs or Deans of the Colleges; 20 percent, Affirmative Action Officers; 17 percent Deans/Chairs of Arts and Sciences/Humanities; and 7 percent, Deans of Education. At the time of response, 51 percent of all respondents had held their "current position" for five years or less.

As for "previous positions," 28 percent were Professors/Instructors; 26 percent, Deans/Chairs; 16 percent, Vice Presidents of Academic Affairs; 7 percent, Associate Deans; 3 percent, Office Managers; 2 percent Affirmative Action Officers; and 18 percent, other. Forty-six percent of all respondents had held their previous position for five years of less.

TABLE 1
Demographic Frequencies
N = 122

	Variables											
	Current Position		Previous Position		Promoted Within		Hired from Outside		Black		White	
Title	(N)	(%)	(N)	(%)	(N)	(%)	(N)	(%)	(N)	(%)	(N)	(%)
President	26	21.3	1	0.8	12	10	13	11			25	21.0
V.P.A.A. (Academic Dean)	25	20.5	19	15.6	16	13	9	7	1	0.8	23	19.0
A.A.O.	24	19.7	2	1.6	21	17	3	2	5	4.0	19	16.0
Dean/Chair Business	21	17.2										
Dean/Chair Arts & Science	18	14.8	30	24.6	28	23	15	12	1	0.8	43	35.0
Dean/Chair Education	8	6.6										
Prof. Inst.			32	26.0								
Associate Dean			8	6.6								
Office Manager			3	2.5								
Other			27	23.0								

Note: The totals for "Promoted Within," "Hired From Outside," and the race columns do not equal the total number (122) since 5 persons indicated "no response" to these items.

63

Of the total sample of administrators, 67 percent had held their previous position within the system and 33 percent held their previous position outside the system. Forty-two percent currently held positions at two year institutions, 47 percent at four year institutions, and 11 percent at universities. With regard to race, 7 percent were black and 93 percent were white.

Results

Several Likert scale items based on measures of "strongly agree" to "strongly disagree," as well as open-ended items, were used as attitudinal indicators to gauge perceptions, opinions, and suggestions regarding recruitment, retention, impact, hiring efforts, salaries, incentives, and opportunities for merit, with respect to black faculty. The responses pertaining to these various aspects are presented in Table 2 and are discussed below.

From an *attitudinal perspective,* an overwhelming majority of administrators surveyed indicate that they are either in favor of increasing the number of black faculty, perceive other administrators to be in favor of actively recruiting black faculty, or perceive such recruitment to be appropriate (91–95%). They acknowledge, by an overwhelming majority, that the numbers of black faculty do not exceed sufficiency (95%). They also acknowledge that institutions within the system have been successful, to some extent, in recruiting black faculty in a wide range of disciplines. It is interesting to note, however, that, aside from the broad areas of Humanities and Social Sciences, the specific discipline referred to with high frequency is Developmental Studies—an area with a high proportion of non-tenure, temporary, and part-time positions.

The techniques perceived as most successful in the recruitment of black faculty also encompass a wide range of activities, the most popular of which are networking and making personal contacts at meetings or conventions (31%), contacts from black faculty or community leaders (16%), and the use of advertisements, letters or multi-media, targeted appeals (16%). Among a wide range of responses, those factors most commonly perceived as influential in successful recruitment were salary (24%), and job description (role), challenge or tenure (15%). Although many viable approaches and reasons for successful recruitment of black faculty have been cited, a majority of respondents perceived no hiring discrimination in favor of black faculty, nor did the majority perceive any internal obstacles to minority recruitment. However, the members of the academic community most commonly identified as obstacles were faculty (16%) and chairpersons (8%).

In contrast to the overwhelming indication that recruitment and increase of black faculty were positively favored, opinions regarding the actual presence of black faculty show some decrease in the intensity of favorable responses. Although administrators did not perceive minority hiring in compliance with federal mandates to be detrimental to the quality of services, the intensity of favorable opinions did shift from "strongly agree" to "agree."

A majority of administrators perceived no discomfort for non-black faculty working with black faculty. The retention strategies most frequently cited as successful were fair treatment, respect, acceptance (28%), and opportunities for advancement (28%).

In spite of respondents' overwhelmingly high rate of approval of the increase in minority recruitment, re-

TABLE 2
Frequency of All Administrative Attitudinal Indicators Regarding Black Faculty Recruitment and Retention
(N = 122)

Proposition	Strongly Agree		Agree		Responses Disagree		Strongly Disagree	
	(N)	(%)*	(N)	(%)*	(N)	(%)*	(N)	(%)*
Increase is Aid to Education	53	45	59	50	5	4	2	2
Others are in favor of Active Recruitment	56	46	58	48	6	5	2	2
Active Recruitment is Unfair	3	3	7	7	50	41	61	50
More than enough at this institution	4	3	3	3	48	39	67	55
Federal Mandates have lowered Quality	1	1	6	5	64	57	41	37
My institution discriminates for blacks	2	2	22	19	56	47	39	33
Majority faculty is uncomfortable	1	1	8	7	50	42	59	50
Increase permanent, full-time, tenured faculty**	27	23	43	37	34	29	13	11

Goals clearly, consistently, stated at all levels	55	45	50	41	14	12	3	3
Institution successful in meeting goals	13	11	42	36	52	44	10	9
Salary for blacks competitive and commensurate	55	47	51	44	9	8	2	2
Should change selection of search committees	6	5	20	17	73	62	18	15
Salary increment where high number of black students	5	4	34	28	63	52	20	16
Salary increments where low cultural/environmental support	8	7	44	37	49	41	18	15
More inclusion on academic committees	16	14	63	56	29	26	4	4
Are provided enough research time	40	40	54	6	6	6	1	1
Are provided meaningful opportunity for service	57	48	56	47	5	4	2	2

*(Percentages have been rounded)
**This item does not apply exclusively to black faculty

sponse to the idea of hiring more permanent, full-time, tenure track faculty at their own institutions indicated a considerably lower rate of approval (60%). In addition, a considerably low number of respondents (47%) perceived success at achieving the minority recruitment goals that a majority (86%) indicated were clearly and consistently stated at all administrative levels. Only a very small percentage of administrators perceived the major responsibility for minority faculty hiring to exist at "all levels" of their institution (4%). In comparison, only a slightly higher percentage of respondents held the opinion that major responsibility should be placed at "all levels" (10%).

A majority of administrators indicated that no change seemed necessary in the selection and designation of search committees (77%); and there was no considerable difference between the first and second place choices for those who should hold major responsibility regarding minority hiring issues, (Chair/Head and Vice President for Academic Affairs—48%), and those who were identified as currently holding such responsibilities (Chair/Head and V.P.A.A.—53%).

An overwhelming majority of respondents held the opinion that black faculty were offered salaries competitive and commensurate with their expertise. More administrators agreed with the idea of offering prospective black faculty additional increments in salary where there were minimal cultural and environmental support systems than in situations where the faculty member could offer a black perspective to substantial numbers of black students.

Although a majority indicated that more black faculty should be included in the processes of vital academic committees, many respondents felt that these faculty members were given enough time and opportunity for research and service.

An *activity awareness perspective* provides interesting information as can be observed in Table 3. In contrast to many of the overwhelmingly supportive responses in favor of recruitment and retention of black faculty, a majority of respondents indicate a lack of awareness of any particular programs or efforts toward these purposes on their own campuses. The effort least familiar to administrators was the existence of black faculty organizations (77%), next, programs geared toward sensitization of majority faculty (60%), and then, curriculum and/ or course offerings with a black focus (52%), visits to recruit outside the system (48%), and invitations for potential candidates to familiarize themselves with the system (32%).

Interestingly, the area of activity which was indicated to have the highest rate of participation, invitations to potential candidates (35%), was also the activity which was perceived to be unsuccessful by the greatest percentage of respondents (18%). (The data do not provide for an indication of whether perceived lack of success was due to rejection of invitations or to eventual failure to recruit individuals who accept such invitations.)

It should be noted that it was, to a great extent, the responsibility or option of white administrators to be aware of and involved in activities supportive of black faculty since the number of black administrators was extremely minimal or virtually non-existent at those institutions within the system where there was also a dire scarcity of black faculty.

The *interview schedule* was administered to survey participants at a) three institutions identified as having a high percentage of black faculty as compared to other

TABLE 3

Activity Awareness/Involvement Indicators by Administrative Position for Two Activities

Activity (Visits)	Level of *Response	President	V.P.A.A. (or equal)	A.A.O.	Dean of Bus.	Dean of Arts & Sci.	Dean of Ed.
				Title/Position			
Outside of the System	1	7	7	13	13	11	6
	2	12	13	6	5	3	1
	3	5	1	1	1	0	0
	4	0	1	2	0	2	1
Invitations to the System	1	3	5	10	11	7	2
	2	3	1	8	3	3	1
	3	13	10	4	3	8	3
	4	5	8	2	3	1	2

*1—Unaware
2—Aware did not Participate
3—Participated/Effort Successful
4—Participated/Effort Unsuccessful

institutions in the system—excluding the traditionally black and b) at three institutions identified as having comparatively low percentages of black faculty. The total number of institutions (six) included a cross-section of types in terms of location (rural, urban), size, and level of degree programs.

A total of 28 administrators were interviewed covering each of the six key positions that were targeted in the survey. The following is a comparison of responses between those administrators with high percentages of black faculty (HPBFs) and those with low percentages of black faculty (LPBFs).

In response to *"In what ways has hiring black faculty impacted upon the morale of your institution"?*, HPBFs and LPBFs gave equal numbers of positive comments; HPBFs gave four negative comments, interestingly, LPBFs gave no negative comments. Samples follow.

HPBFs comments:

Positive: "good role models for whites as well as blacks/ increased enrollment of black students/ it completes the curriculum/ good role models for students as well as faculty / serves to dissipate stereotypes/ brings varied cultural perspective."

Negative: "some see as reverse discrimination/ white faculty initially felt put upon—some searches were not productive/ no particular resentment except returning some searches or shutting them down/ generally white faculty has been non-chalant/ one may have created difficulty because of strong personality."

Neutral: "no adverse effects, no problems, no particular impact"

LPBFs comments:

Positive: "positive for faculty and students/mentoring for students/eliminates ethnocentric experience—move toward real world/ expression of appreciation for role models/ positive stand toward progress/ powerful impact/ good liaisons.''

Negative: (none)

Neutral: ''no especially bad responses/ no protest/ no problem with student body.''

When asked *"What major selling points does your institution have to offer all prospective faculty,"*? LPBFs gave almost as many positive comments as HPBFs, LPBFs two negative comments, and HPBFs no negative comments. Samples follow.

HPBFs comments:

Positive: ''proximity to metropolitan (urban) area/ growth potential/ good salaries/ good budgets/ strategies for future/ dedicated faculty/ good housing/ good academic reputation/ small town flavor/ 'esprit de corp'/ academic and professional freedom/ good graduates/ varied lifestyles in surrounding community/ good promotion record/ good campus setting/ young active faculty.''

LPBFs comments:

Positive: ''scholarship/ environment conducive to attracting diversified pool/ nice college town/ good place to raise children/ good reputation/ good resources/ merit-oriented system/ personal touch/ political pull/ stimulating colleagues/ reasonable cost of living/ relatively small/ not a cow-college.''

Negative: ''no great selling points/ enrollments down— not as much to offer.'' ''none'' or that the challenges would be ''the same.'' Samples follow.

HPBFs comments:

Negative: ''perceived isolation/ naivete of student body—no exposure/ lack of understanding of white faculty/ less merit value on black faculty ties with community/ hoping to be faculty member with all rights and privileges—will be seen as a black person in the class-room—challenge to be twice as good—cannot be average/ suspect that students will challenge to be better than other faculty/ fundamentalism embedded in racial tension/ veiled prejudice/ not many black faculty/ superficial acceptance."

Neutral: "salary/ dealing with diverse student body—vocationally oriented and underprepared/ how to find comparative advantage/ teaching loads/ tremendous competition."

LPBFs comments:

Negative: "process of gaining more "critical mass of black faculty" and educated blacks in the community affects the perception of possibility for adjustment/ trouble with research/ challenging demand to be "super-black"/ lack of black middle-class—no social supports/ to be able to rise above prejudice in the community/ proximity to area with racial tension."

Neutral: "to survive the workload and committees/ large town-small town (depending on orientation)/ we have faculty housing."

It should be noted that, although some institutions within the system have a higher percentage of black faculty than others—excluding the HBCUs—those with a high percentage still have a considerably disproportionate representation of black faculty in terms of population demographics in general.

From a *one-on-one interview perspective,* administrators of institutions with high percentages of black faculty (HPBFs) and those at institutions with low percentages of black faculty (LPBFs) differed most in their responses to the question of how black faculty had impacted upon the morale of their institution. Where HPBFs gave some responses reflecting negative experiences and LPBFs gave no negative indications, it is possible that LPBF administrators did not have knowledge of black faculty interaction, had no black faculty during their tenure, or did not wish to create a negative image. Overall, interview responses from HPBF and LPBF administrators were more alike than they were different. Responses given were also in keeping with the nature of answers to similar items on the system-wide survey, with the exception that there was a substantially greater proportion of negative reflections which were probably more realistic.

Finally, a finding secondary to the intended focus is a disproportionate representation of minorities among the administrative ranks within the system, no doubt, a contributing factor to the disproportion of minority faculty. There are a limited number of role models for existing black faculty and a limited number of liaisons for a recruitment network. It should be noted that although there are relatively few minorities within the system, there have been many opportunities to hire minority administrators, since 33 percent of all respondents were hired into their current position from outside of the system. It was also found that a considerable majority of the Affirmative Action Officers are white, allowing for the possibility that, although these individuals may be well versed of their responsibilities, they may not be sensitive to the needs of prospective or existing avenues for optimizing the recruitment network for black faculty candidates.

Conclusion

Since a number of respondents either felt that no recruitment techniques could be considered successful for hiring black faculty (''none''), had no answer to the related question, or gave no response (12%), it appears that administrators would benefit from sharing a pool of information on techniques found successful by a majority of their peers. A wide array of viable suggestions have been provided which account for the clinical/academic aspects as well as the humanistic factors perceived to be critical to prospective black faculty.

The diversity of perceptions, opinions, and suggestions pertaining to recruitment and retention techniques, indicates that there are no set formulas for the successful hiring of black faculty. The strategies that are most successful for any particular institution are most likely a function of the type of school (level of degrees), its location (urban, rural), its reputation and its needs. (It is interesting to note that many respondents have acknowledged that the nature of the student body and students' ability levels, as well as the school's reputation (locally, regionally, and nationally) are perceived as factors influential in the successful recruitment and retention of black faculty. In other instances, problems with housing have been cited as deterrents—a function of the locale of the institution. There appears to be a need to invest more effort into revising and improving strategies for recruitment and retention of black faculty since responses suggest that, although related goals and objectives are clearly and consistently stated at all administrative levels, there has been less than substantial success at meeting such goals.

A considerable percentage (45%) of respondents had ''no answer'' to how black faculty impacted upon the morale of their institutions, perceived no impact, or did not respond. This can be interpreted as an indication that either there were no black faculty at respondents' institutions, there were very few black faculty at some institutions, some administrators were unaware of the nature or quality of black faculty interactions on their campus, or the presence of black faculty was not perceived as having any particular significance.

Since only a very small percentage of administrators perceived the major responsibility for minority faculty hiring to exist at "all levels" of their institution and only a slightly higher percentage of respondents held the opinion that major responsibility should be placed at "all levels," perhaps there is not enough involvement of each individual who holds some capacity to affect policy, make leadership decisions and set the tone for the agenda of the academic community regarding minority affairs. Although there must be an ultimate authority, there is obviously a need for a more carefully orchestrated and structured recruitment and retention plan which would require the efforts of a substantial cross-section of participants.

Where the data indicate that a recruitment activity participated in to the greatest extent was also perceived as least successful, it appears that there is a need to carefully assess such efforts to determine how they might be improved. Where there are substantial indications that less familiar activities yield a ratio of perceived success comparable to those activities which are more popular, these efforts should also be carefully assessed to determine how they might be improved. Efforts to visit campuses outside of the system to inform potential candidates deserve the same careful monitoring and revision as efforts to invite potential candidates to the system.

With regard to power, leadership style, decision making and bringing about change, it is evident that some administrators have exercised the authority to assess a search as "non-productive" if no black faculty candidate emerged with a favorable recommendation, have decided to either "return some searches" or "shut them down," and have, thereby, either brought about change in black faculty hiring or, at least, set the non-traditional example. In terms of planning and goal setting, some administrators have, at least expressed a vision of the role that diversity plays in the pursuit and delivery of educational services, have demonstrated a sensitivity toward considerations and realities of particular concern to prospective and existing black faculty, and have assessed those features of their institution and its surrounding environment which may be perceived as either strengths or weaknesses by potential candidates. They have accounted for the negative as well as positive elements that create the 'gestalt' of the status and direction of black faculty recruitment and retention.

Respondents' Recommendations

The following is a set of recommendations which have been quoted from the suggestions generated by survey participants. These recommendations have been selected from the total sample on the basis that they are the most specific, most timely, or most aggressive ideas which have been offered.

• Provide faculty housing on campuses in isolated areas or homogeneous communities and reserve a certain number of minority recruits.
• Create a data pool which immediately alerts all schools in the system if an invited black candidate does not get or accept the first position for which they are considered.

• Create more vita banks, some discipline-specific, and support more consortium efforts to work with industry and corporate structure to create scholarships for the Ph.D.

• Adopt the Ohio state plan in which universities "grow their own" out of doctoral programs.

• Demonstrate a strong sense of commitment from the top which projects beyond the OCR requirements.

• Upgrade salary structure (particularly for junior colleges) and provide more travel funds for prospective candidates.

• Support recruitment visits from the Central Office and the efforts of the Consortium and advise a department that it can retrieve a retirement position if it brings in a black visiting professor.

• Establish a structured effort to provide "buddies" for new black faculty from the pool of existing black faculty and other committed individuals.

• Adopt the National Science Foundation model which holds positions in abeyance so that departments compete for a good black candidate, uses visiting scholars and provides incentives for their commitment, and recruits from quality groups where the top-ten from a larger pool are considered equal in quality first and race becomes secondary.

• Provide more funding for positions and more support for black faculty pursuing the terminal degree.

Researcher's Recommendations

The following is a list of recommendations generated by the researcher which are based on the collective findings of the survey. These recommendations have been offered as possible solutions to specific problems or deficiencies which appear to be most pervasive across institutions and administrative levels within the system.

• Monitor and balance the number and ratio of non-tenure, temporary, and part-time positions which are made available and are offered to black candidates as compared to white candidates within departments.

• Conduct sensitivity workshops for faculty and department chairs/heads to aid understanding, identify common goals and benefits, and allay fears and misconceptions associated with the inclusion of black faculty.

• Create centers for research on culture and ethnicity which attract black scholars and provide the black perspective necessary to foster understanding for black and white faculty and students and provide a support base for black faculty and students.

• Monitor and balance the number and ratio of administrative positions which are made available and are offered to black candidates as compared to white candidates for specific positions.

• Engage and monitor participation in or response to all activities and efforts related to black faculty recruitment and retention at all administrative levels.

• Create a checklist of procedures listing several alternatives for each objective which every individual involved in recruitment and retention must respond to and submit before each recruitment/retention effort is resolved.

• Establish a category for evaluation of black faculty recruitment and retention in every institutional effectiveness assessment conducted and reported within the system.

These sets of recommendations constitute both the

emic and etic viewpoints of solutions to identified problems—the respondents' (administrators') perceptions of and reactions to the circumstances in question and the researcher's perceptions of and reactions to the circumstances in question. It is hoped that these sets of recommendations are used in conjunction with one another. Both of these lists serve distinct but integrally related purposes. The respondents often have a first hand view of specific and on-going problems and deficiencies unique to their particular environments and observations, and the researcher has had the opportunity to develop a collective perspective of the variety of perceptions, opinions, and suggestions characteristic of the issue system-wide.

References

Buckley, John J. and Feldbaum, Eleanor G. Faculty influences on black recruitment and retention in schools of nursing. Maryland University, College Park. Program of Health Services Delivery, 1979. ED181159.

Hellweg, Susan A. and Churchman, David A. Sponsored research as a solution to four pervasive problems in graduate education. Association for Institutional Research Forum, 1979. ED174125.

Henry, Philip N. Affirmative action: A concern in higher education administration. The Organization and Administration of Higher Education, 1980. ED210408.

Kentucky Commission on Human Rights. Number and percent of black faculty at state universities decline from 1979 to 1981. Staff Report 82-10. Louisville, Kentucky, 1982. ED237608.

Nickson, Sheila J. Status of minority professionals on majority campuses: Saviors, Victims, or Survivors? Paper presented at the National Association for Equal Opportunity in Higher Education, Washington, D.C., 1982. ED256832.

Simmons, Howard. Transition or transformation? Annual Report of the Executive Director of the Commission on Higher Education. Commission on Higher Education, Philadelphia, Pennsylvania Middle States Association of Colleges and Schools, 1984.

University of Georgia. Higher Education Staff Information EEO-6 Report. Equal Opportunity Commission, Office for Civil Rights, 1985.

Weinstein, Minna. Transition or transformation? Annual Report of the Executive Director of the Commission on Higher Education. Commission on Higher Education, Philadelphia, Pennsylvania Middle States Association of Colleges and Schools, 1984.

NAFEO

The National Association for Equal Opportunity in Higher Education, (NAFEO), founded in October, 1969, was formed as a voluntary, independent association by historically and predominantly black colleges and universities. It is organized to articulate the need for a higher education system where race, income, and previous education are not determinants of either the quantity or quality of higher education. This is an association of those colleges and universities which are not only committed to this ultimate goal, but are now fully committed in terms of their resources, human and financial, to achieving that goal.

The Association proposes, through collective efforts of its membership, to promote the widest possible sensitivity to the complex factors involved in and the institutional commitment required for creating successful higher education programs for students from groups buffeted by racism and neglected by economic, educational and social institutions of America.

To achieve this goal, NAFEO has determined the following priorities:

1. To provide a unified framework representing historically black colleges and similarly situated institutions in their attempt to continue as viable forces in American society;

2. To build the case for securing increased support from federal agencies, philanthropic foundations and other sources;

3. To increase the active participation of Black in the leadership of educational organizations together with memberships on Federal boards and commissions relating to education; and

4. To provide detailed, continuing yearly analyses of constructive information about these colleges and to use that information to help the public develop and maintain a sensitivity to the overall needs of these institutions of higher education.

NAFEO's aim is to increase the flow of students from minority and economically deprived families, mostly Black, into the mainstream of our society.

In carrying out its four major specific objectives, NAFEO serves as a—

1. Voice for Historically Black Colleges

2. Clearinghouse of Information on Black Colleges

3. Coordinator in Black Higher Education

4. Presidential Resource.

The National Association for Equal Opportunity in Higher Education represents the historically and predominantly black colleges and universities of this nation.

There are some 117 NAFEO institutions, consisting of private 2-year and 4-year institutions, public 2-year and 4-year institutions, as well as graduate and professional schools located in fourteen southern states, six northern states, four mid-west and western states, the Virgin Islands and the District of Columbia. These institutions enroll upwards of 250,000 students and graduate more than 40,000 students annually with undergraduate, graduate and professional degrees. Since 1966, these institutions have awarded a half million undergraduate, graduate and professional degrees. They are the providers of equal educational opportunity with attainment and productivity for thousands of students.

NAFEO'S RESEARCH ADVISORY COMMITTEE

87

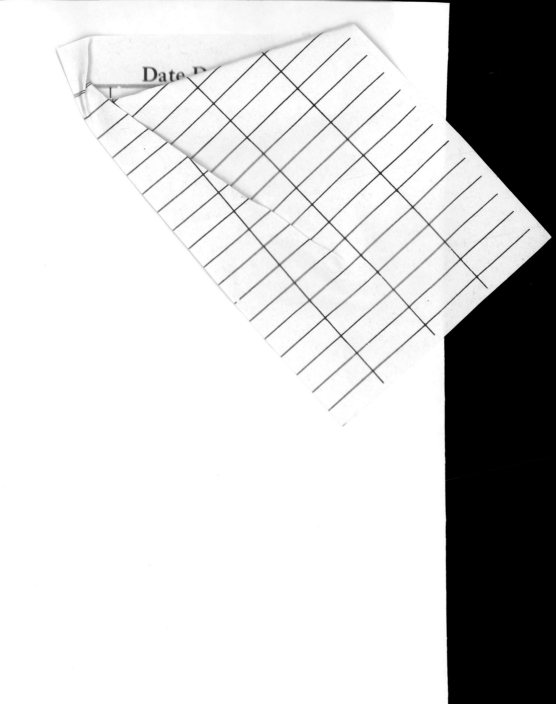

Date D